Magic and Management

Magic and Management

◆

Developing Executive Potentials

W. E. Bjur and G. R. Caravantes

iUniverse, Inc.
New York Lincoln Shanghai

Magic and Management
Developing Executive Potentials

iUniverse, Inc.

For information address:
iUniverse, Inc.
2021 Pine Lake Road, Suite 100
Lincoln, NE 68512
www.iuniverse.com

Porto Alegre, Brazil
Sacramento, CA
October, 1996
August, 2000
February, 2003

©Translation: Wesley E. Bjur, Sacramento, CA 1996, 2000

Published by FACTEC, Fundação de Apoio à Ciência, Tecnología, Educação e Cultura Porto Alegre, RS, Brasil

ISBN: 0-595-27104-9

Printed in the United States of America

to Rejane and Dottie, with our love.

Contents

Part II   *Managing Oneself*

Part III   Managing the Transpersonal

Preface to the First (Portuguese) Edition[1]

by Luiz Sergio Coelho Sampaio
Brazilian Academy of Philosophy
São Paulo, Brazil 1996

Administrative and organizational knowledge does not exist in the simple modality of a basic science, as would be the case of physics, biology, psychology and many others. Its object, organizations—a complex of installations, equipment, and persons of different formations, abilities, and responsibilities, acting in coordination with a view of specific ends and a clearly defined mission—by its very nature gives rise to the mobilization of multiple sciences, knowledge, and practices. It is for this reason that a serious work in this domain requires of its authors a wide cultural base, including a minimum of familiarity with what has been happening in innumerable and dynamic forefronts of knowledge. There is also required a dramatic capacity of selection and synthesis that will protect them from falling into a disoriented eclecticism or in a mere "book of recipes."

The authors of *Management and Magic: Learning to ReAdminister Your Personal Life* pass, with room to spare, this severe pretest of quality. The work seeks its sources and fundamentals wherever they can be found—in philosophy, in quantum and relativist modern physics, in critical sociology, in anthropology, in the multiple and practical psychological conceptualizations, and in much more—paring down, however, and adapting them, as necessary, to administrative concerns. As a result, we are here presented with a variety of administrative and organizational paradigms, and convinced to choose neither this nor that one, but rather to assume a decidedly strategic attitude in the face of all of them. We have no doubt that this is one of the best, if not the best and most daring book in this vein that has come into our hands in the arena of an administrative specialization.

---

1. Published by Makron Books in São Paulo, Brazil in 1996 with the title: *Magia e Gestão*. Translation from Portuguese by Wesley E. Bjur, Sacramento, CA.

There are innumerable moments of excellence in this book by Caravantes and Bjur. Not having here enough space to explain and comment on all of them, we select only two that, in our view, are among the best. Both are found in Chapter 7, at its beginning and near the end (*Thinking about Life…What Does it Mean to be Rational?* and "*Learning to Learn*") Here, the authors base themselves initially on the best of German sociology—Weber and Mannheim, followed by others from the Frankfurt School, especially Marcuse and Horkheimer—to characterize modernity in terms of the conflict between substantive (that of *ends*) and functional/utilitarian rationality (that of *means*) pointing out the hegemony imposed by the latter over the former. At the global or macro-economic level (Karl Polanyi), or at the impresarial or micro-economic level (Simon), we observe that there prevails a doctrine of the absolutization of the market, which means, the sacralization of the *means* to the detriment of the *ends*, not leaving the least room for consideration of matters of an ethical order. According to Voegelin, cited by these authors, the society has entered into a true process of "derailment" resulting in a complete lack of compassion for others. Who can deny this sad portrait of actuality in our world?

The authors do not deny, nor could they, the successes of the utilitarianism cited, mentioning as an example the United States, the first country to achieve reasonable conditions of living for a quasi-totality of their more than 260 million inhabitants, including the fact that they have done this with less than 3% of their active population dedicated to agriculture. On this point they make it evident that the "Second Wave," that is, industrialism, which itself consumed a previous agricultural revolution, the great American revolution following the War of Secession [Revolutionary War]. In the meantime, the result of the hegemonic prevalence of functional rationality over substantive rationality could not be but another sign of disaster. In the name of efficiency they arrive at the standardization of thought and action; they educate homogenous human beings suited for production; their media works to achieve a uniformization of opinions among people. Perhaps we [i.e., Brazil] shall need to pass through all this, they suggest, but they leave it clear that such an outcome is not sufficient for the authors themselves.

The last item in **Part II: Chapter 7** takes us to the world of learning. We are there alerted that the newborn child does not have to worry about "learning to learn." To the contrary, he is born already an excellent master at learning. It is the educational system—and, equally, our impresarial systems of training—that act to dull this naïve ability, of inestimable value. This argues the need of "learning to learn," because it involves learning to *unlearn*. "*To learn new forms of encoun-*

tering the world and its problems will involve the unlearning of habits and values that we have maintained for many years, in order to see them substituted by other logics based upon a different complex of beliefs." And this is what they are proposing: that we relearn other logics—logics which we recognize we are born with which have become familiar—but which our utilitarian culture, in order to impose itself, has needed to emphasize. In summary, the authors have reason: in order to "learn to learn" as adults, it is necessary to relearn how to learn, being prepared first to unlearn whatever that might entail.

To conclude, we would like to commend the satisfaction it was for us to read, and later write a *Preface* to the work of Caravantes and Bjur, and to affirm, with all conviction, that a majority of the administrators of medium and large national enterprises, both public and private, should make the effort to read, to understand, and to discuss with their peers this book (even though they might not agree with everything). With this, the quality of Brazilian management will experience a significant qualitative leap for the better, something which no "canned" foreign product, in substitution, would be able to provide. For such, it is hardly necessary that we Brazilians, despite circumstances so adverse—we must admit—shall find at the end our self-esteem.

Preface to the English Language Edition

Management and Magic is the fourth book of the *ReAdministration* series. In it we propose to advance and enrich the life of individuals and managers of organizations, based upon ideas included in the conceptual framework we have labeled *ReAdministration*.

In 1996 we published in São Paulo *ReAdministração em Ação: A Prática da Mudança Rumo a Sucesso (ReAdministration In Action: The Practice of Change Oriented Toward Success)*[1]. In it, the authors proposed a conceptual framework for administration labeled "ReAdministration" to indicate a schema to be preferred over what was proposed by Hammer and Champy in *"Reengineering the Corporation"*[2] and by David Osborne and Ted Gaebler, *"Reinventing Government."*[3] In practice, after a couple of years the idea of *"Reengineering the Corporation"* had come to be synonymous with massive layoffs in large U. S. corporations such as Ford, IBM, General Electric, and others.

When "reengineering/reinventing" began to be applied to corporations in Brazil (the home of author Caravantes) with its massive layoffs and no social net to catch them, Caravantes decided that there had to be better alternatives than *reengineering* to recommend to public and private sector managers in Brazil. So was born a broader framework for a management theory that incorporates society-wide values beyond mere technical or engineering efficiency. He called it *ReAdministration*.

In its name, it carries the idea that renovations in administrative practice are always necessary, but what experience has proven to be good administrative practices should not be abandoned in favor of short-term, draconian "reinventions" that lose sight of long-term objectives of organization and society and their

1.   Geraldo Caravantes and Wesley Bjur, *ReAdministração em Ação: A Prática da Mudança Rumo a Sucesso.* São Paulo: Makron Books do Brasil, 1996,
2.   Michael Hammer and James Champy, *Reengineering the Corporation: A Manifesto for Business Revolution.* NY: Harper Collins Books, 1993.
3.   David Osborne and Ted Gaebler, *Reinventing Government: How the Entrepreneurial Spirit Is Transforming the Public Sector.* NY: Penguin Books, 1991

impact on the individual. Parting from a premise that solution of problems is possible only by means of *better* administration, but not *traditional* administration as we see it normally practiced, we proposed rather a *renewed* administration as the solution, one which we labeled *ReAdministration,* and which is defined as:

> *a way to manage contemporary organizations in a manner so as to achieve efficient, effectual, and effective organizations, whose employees are satisfied and suitably recompensed for what they achieve. By **efficient**, we mean productive organizations; by **effectual**, we refer to achieving planned objectives in a systematic and continued way; and by **effective** we mean they hold in consideration their public responsibility, nurturing an ethic about the way they do business.* [4]

The *ReAdministration* framework seeks for an integration of *good society/good organizations/good individuals.* We pointed out that the survival of organizations in a turbulent context depends on flexible structures, capable of adaptation; not merely *reactive* adaptation, but rather, *proactive* responses to changes in an intelligent and strategic manner.

As time passed, it became clear that an enhanced guide for higher-level managers was needed to affirm the style of management recommended by the ReAdministration framework. The fundamental idea has been to transcend theoretical models which are concerned with mere efficiency and efficacy of organizations, and to introduce other concerns which include *effectiveness;* here defined as emphasizing social and ethical responsibilities along with the search for individual satisfaction.

The book introduces and advocates *paradigm competence* as a requisite for modern, high-level management. Paradigm is understood as a culturally provided "big picture" framework for understanding how the world is, and how things work. Unless the manager has lived abroad, and/or learned other languages, it is probable that s/he possesses a single working paradigm, most likely one called "the positive science" paradigm.

To broaden the conceptual perspective of high-level managers, we begin *Magic and Management* with an overview of the "positive science" paradigm, followed by three additional, alternative ways of looking at the world; the quantum physics, mystical, and existential paradigms. We hope that we have been successful in explaining to readers why we believe this is important for modern managers.

---

4.   Caravantes and Bjur, *ReAdministração em Ação.* São Paulo: Makron Books do Brasil, 1996, p.2

Management And Magic

❖

Introduction

WHAT DOES MAGIC HAVE TO DO WITH MANAGEMENT?

The reader can well ask, "What does *magic* have to do with *management?*" "Magic" is usually understood as some event or experience that seems impossible to explain by commonly understood rational or physical laws. In contrast, "management" is usually taught as the application of *rational* principles to the coordination of human activities in organizations we create and work in.

What will the reader benefit from reading this book?

In contrast to the technical rationality that constitutes the core curricula of schools of management, the authors have observed that much of the leadership expected of *senior* managers depends upon *extra-rational* capabilities. Hunches, intuitions, feelings that one action is to be preferred over another are examples, for us, of the senior manager making use of the more-than-rational. "Magic" is the word we use to name those talents. Furthermore, the experienced manager who has not developed a talent for the use of this "magic" available in one's unconscious will find his or her career falling short in the upper levels of leadership.

So the title *Magic and Management* was chosen to highlight our belief that the best managers are those who are obviously well-trained in the rational tools of their craft, *but more than that,* they are comfortable in the use of extra-rational potentials, those that mark their leadership as extraordinary.

We know that upper-level executives are often obligated to make important choices and decisions despite insufficient information and an inability to predict future outcomes. Such decisions must necessarily depend on hunches, "gut feel-ings," unconscious hints and intuitions stemming from past experiences.

In later chapters we emphasize the importance of the unconscious in enabling an individual's access to one's infraconscious, extra-rational, or "magic" capabili-ties, along with some contemporary techniques that can be used to enhance them.

Purposes of the Authors

This book is our attempt to develop an understanding of managerial issues and responses that are based upon the premises of the *ReAdministration* framework set forth above in the *Preface to the English Language Edition*.

Clientele: The clientele we have had in mind as we created this book are upper level *executives/administrators,* however defined. In the broadest sense, we write for all those who seek to better manage their lives, to live as happy and integrated human beings. The search for success and happiness is an ultimate goal. Who does not seek this?

We believe that administrators need to have working knowledge of the applied social sciences taught in several areas of academia, including the juridical, eco-nomic, and political sciences, philosophy, and linguistics. We have wanted to cul-tivate a *pragmatic* vision in the treatment of this knowledge. For the authors, *good* knowledge is *useful* knowledge, understanding here knowledge that permits us to live our lives better. Such an option has had direct consequences in our choice of themes, in their prioritization, and in the selective use of examples as an aid to understanding.

Language: We have wanted to avoid jargon and non-standard expressions as much as possible. While we have not been able to dispense entirely with some specialized terms, we have attempted to use language that is deemed to be within the reader's reach. When it has been necessary to open the lexicon of technical language, we have wanted to use an almost journalistic style, as much as possible.

Structure of the book: Following the *Introduction,* **Part I: Paradigms and Management** begins the development of what the authors believe to be an important contribution to advanced management practice—the idea that high level managers need to be competent in several viable paradigms covering the scope of their responsibilities. So we introduce the idea of *paradigm competence,* with examples of four very "big picture" paradigms that currently influence ways of looking at the world. We provide descriptive frameworks for Four Exemplar Paradigms, labeled successively: Positive Science, Quantum Physics, Oriental

Mysticism, and Existentialism. Creativity and innovation derive almost exclusively from such competence. A high number of creative innovations are the result of borrowing ideas from other contexts, other paradigms. Since we are builders of our own reality, a competence in creating new paradigms for ordering new realities is very important to high-level managers.

Part II, Managing Oneself, is concentrated on how to "know oneself" which explains the main divisions of this section; Managing the Conscious, Managing the Unconscious, and Managing the Conscious/Unconscious Interface. This analysis of the individual always maintains ReAdministration as the basic conceptual framework, which forces us to work simultaneously with a micro-organizational and macro-societal vision, making constant references to both of these levels. We propose the use of traditional scientific frameworks in collaboration with less orthodox forums in the interests of a better understanding of the individual, who is simultaneously actor and spectator, agent and client, of his own life. Among less orthodox forums, we include a discussion on access to the unconscious via hypnosis.

Part III, Managing the Transpersonal, adds something new, something "beyond" the rational elements of the mind, to highlight the "magic" parts of high-level management talents that are a main theme of this book. It deals with elements or influences beyond the individual that are called the spiritual.

There is also a chapter on the "magic" of overcoming personal crises in transcendent encounters with some force or energy normally beyond our reach.

Concluding paragraphs suggest the need for the manager to be concerned about happiness, happiness for the manager personally, as well as some responsibility the manager has for the happiness of the working group, along with an expected concern for the effectiveness of the organization.

The Challenges Facing Contemporary Managers

Part of our premise is that the *good society* is not a gift, but is rather a process of collective creation in which *good* organizations (remember that we live in an organizational society) will be their main support. The authors believe that the *legal fictions* we call organizations are the creation of individuals who act in them, most especially, their leadership. And, reasoning backwards, we do not see how to obtain a healthy society without healthy organizations, neither do we see organizations of high productivity being peopled by unhappy individuals who are under-utilized, where it is impossible for them to achieve their potential. We share the vision of Aldous Huxley, who writes, *"the objective of human life is to maximize individual potentialities, and in the best possible way, to create a society which facilitates that maximization.*[1]

Abraham Maslow also affirms "the achievement of the highest human desires is possible—in mass terms—only through *good conditions*. Or, more directly, good human beings generally need a good society in which they will be able to develop."[2]

Beginning from these premises, we recognize the interdependence and integration of the elements *good society/good organizations/good individuals*, and the benefits of a management necessary to guarantee that interdependence and integration. In *Magic and Management* we have wanted to contribute to the development of a management style and practice that achieves these ends for the individual as well as for the organization. We should not forget that it is the individuals who are the creators of the organization that employs them, and renovations must be conceived with concern for those individuals in mind.

Untapped Mental Potential

It is commonly affirmed that humans do not utilize more than about 10% of their mental capacity, leaving the remaining 90% untouched. Of course, these percentages have not been measured exactly, they merely attempt to indicate that human beings possess an untouched potential, many times superior to their mental capacity actually in use.

Two questions come immediately to mind:

1. if, while utilizing a minimum of our potential mental stock we have achieved a modicum of civilization, how much better might it be if we were able to use a bit more of this latent potential?

2. What can we do to transform this sub-utilized potential into a more effective capacity for the improvement of our lives?

It is the sincere desire of the authors that *Magic and Management* helps the reader to find answers to these questions. We wish you useful and good reading.

---

1.   Aldous Huxley, *A Situação Humana*. Rio de Janeiro: Globo, 1985, p.63
2.   Abraham Maslow, *The Farther Reaches of Human Nature*. NY: Penguin Books, 1976, p.7

PART I

Paradigms and Management

Chapter 1:
Paradigm Competence: A Contemporary Necessity

The Idea of a Paradigm

> *We observe that a scientific community, upon acquiring a paradigm, acquires also the criteria by which to choose the problems that, within the accepted paradigm, it is possible to assume that there are possible solutions. In large measure, these are the only problems which the community will admit as scientific, or will encourage its members to solve. Other problems, along with some that were accepted earlier, now come to be rejected as metaphysical or as being part of some other discipline. They may even be rejected as being too difficult to merit spending time on them. Thus, a paradigm may deflect the scientific community from some relevant social problems that are not reducible to the form of the current puzzle, since they cannot be stated in terms compatible with the instruments and concepts provided by the paradigm.*[1]

What you will find in this chapter

1. **The concept of paradigm**

2. **Why paradigms are so important**

3. **The idea of Paradigm Competence; how useful is it?**

4. **Unexamined paradigm assumptions**

---

1. Thomas Kuhn, *The Structure of Scientific Revolutions.* (Chicago: University of Chicago Press, 1962)

Why the Need for Paradigm Competence?

The modern manager increasingly is expected to demonstrate high levels of sophistication and understanding of complex problems. Some of the challenges managers face include the following:

1. **Managing technology.** In today's organizations, managers need to understand and to employ advanced technology in the relentless drive to improve productivity. Technology itself is constantly changing. Advanced technologies often require advanced knowledge paradigms to understand them.

2. **Managing consultants.** The competent manager is expected to make intelligent decisions about which technology to buy, which consultants to trust for technical advice, and when/how to train operating personnel. Conceptual approaches used by consultants vary widely, and it requires some paradigm competence on the part of managers to be able to make wise judgments as to that which is best for the organization.

3. **Managing organizational changes.** Introducing changes in the organization, whether technology-driven, or in reorganizing for better efficiency, requires high skills in the leadership and training of people. Paradigm competence will enable the manager to choose the best explanatory metaphors for communicating the need for change, as well as the expected implications and outcomes for affected employees.

4. **Managing professional personnel.** Sophisticated technology requires better-educated operators, and these expect a more autonomous style of management and more sophisticated leadership. The manager who is prisoner of a single paradigm will be unable to communicate effectively with a technically sophisticated staff.

5. **Managing communications.** A better-educated work force is not well utilized unless managers and employees can clearly communicate with each other and with peers. The easiest and best guarantor of efficient communications is when both parties are aware that they share a similar paradigm, a similar view of how things *are* and how they *function*. A manager who is literate in several conceptual paradigms will find it easier to establish an easy rapport with superiors and subordinates.

6. **Managing imponderables.** There are inevitable imponderables introduced from factors external to the organization. Political leaders change, and new legislation can have serious impacts on revenues, markets, labor costs, and social obligations. Managers need to be able to see the "big picture" from several different points of view.

7. **Managing external events.** Nearly every modern organization is subject to perturbing factors from events occurring perhaps halfway around the globe, now that most of us share in global markets, and receive televised news beamed instantaneously from satellites of unsettling events which can concern both leaders and employees. Manager-leaders who enjoy multi-paradigm competency have the advantage of being able to "see" the events from several different perspectives, and to interpret their meaning to others with greater lucidity.

All in all, modern managers need to be "paradigm-competent"—to be knowledgeable and comfortable in the use of several alternative frames of reference which can aid in making choices and decisions in the face of constantly new challenges.

Paradigms and Paradigm Poverty

The most serious limitations in the search for true knowledge are found in the unconscious, paradigmatic assumptions that pre-define our perceptions. The chaos of immediate impressions takes on order and clarity for us only when we "name" what is being perceived, and so permeate it with associations and qualities from our culture.

—W. Bjur

Paradigm poverty (meaning a limited conceptual repertoire) is a limiting factor in the career development of promising executives. A manager who attempts to fit every problem into a single conceptual mold may have success with a class of problems associated with that framework, but can fail miserably when faced with problems of a different type. Perhaps the single factor most plainly differentiating a manager's skill is the relative richness of his paradigm repertoire when it comes to analyzing and solving a variety of problems.

A *paradigm,* or conceptual framework, may be likened to software used to program a computer. Just as there are different software programs suited to working with different data forms and different types of work, different conceptual frameworks are used for analyzing and resolving problems associated with the design and management of organizations. In today's complex and turbulent political, economic, and technical environments, a successful manager needs to possess a variety of conceptual frameworks to employ as the need arises.

This introductory chapter will give an abbreviated history of the evolution of the major conceptual paradigms that have characterized Eastern and Western civilizations since Aristotle. It will illustrate this evolution with a definition and description of the qualities that characterize four conceptual paradigms. Two have a history of more than 2,500 years, and two have had wide acceptance and growing use in the past century. They are 1) western positive science, 2) eastern mysticism, 3) quantum physics, and 4) existentialism. Positive science and quantum physics have developed with a focus on understanding the material universe, while eastern mysticism and existentialism have focused on a different world view in order to be enlightened, to better understand the meaning of human existence, motivations and behaviors in a changing world.

Grof gives a summary definition of how the word *paradigm* is currently used:

> *[A] paradigm can be defined as a constellation of beliefs, values, and techniques shared by members of a given scientific community. Some paradigms are of a basic philosophical nature and are very general and encompassing, others govern scientific thinking in rather specific and circumscribed areas of research.*[2]

The term *paradigm* was introduced into the modern vocabulary by a science historian, Thomas Kuhn, who became concerned about discrepancies and disagreements among social scientists concerning the application of natural science methods and techniques to studies of human phenomena in the social sciences. Researchers in astronomy, physics and chemistry seemed to share a wide agreement about the nature of what they were studying, how their investigations should be conducted, and the reliability of their findings. The situation was quite different among social scientists, however, where Kuhn noted that there were serious controversies over fundamental problems. After an intensive study in the history of science, in 1962 Kuhn published his groundbreaking work, *The Structure of Scientific Revolutions*,[3] in which he proposed and developed the idea of evolving and competing knowledge frameworks that he labeled "paradigms."

---

2.   Stanislav Grof, *Beyond the Brain.* (NY: State University of New York Press, 1985) p.3

3.   Thomas Kuhn, *The Structure of Scientific Revolutions.* (Chicago: University of Chicago Press, 1962)

Kuhn noted that when a paradigm is accepted by a majority of the scientific community, it becomes a mandatory way of approaching problems. Kuhn labeled this stage as a period of "normal science." Normal science works on an assumption that the scientific community knows what the universe is like. Leading theories define what is possible and what is not possible in this universe. The educational system teaches this view of the world as irrefutable fact to generations of children. Research consists of solving questions that arise as "puzzles" from this recognized way of looking at things.

It can be seen, then, that paradigms have not only an explanatory function, but also a normative one—they tend to define what is possible and what is not possible, along with acceptable and non-acceptable explanations about how the world is constituted and how it functions. In fact, in a period of "normal" science, the scientific community tends to reject and suppress, sometimes at considerable cost, all "novel" explanations because they are seen as subversive to its basic beliefs and commitments.

Scientific Revolutions

Kuhn noted that in the course of western history, normal science has been viewed as a cumulative process; the idea that knowledge builds cumulatively over time as scientists select those problems that can be solved with concepts and instruments already in existence. Therefore, their findings are confirmatory, and "build upon" the well-defined paradigm. However, Kuhn sees an historical pattern of periodic disturbances in this picture of scientific stability and cumulation. From time to time, new discoveries appear which do not fit into the prevailing accounts of how the world is constituted. Faced with a pattern of inconsistent findings, researchers begin to cast about for an alternative way to understand the reality of the cases they observe. Eventually a new way of conceptualizing the scenario, of viewing relationships among elements, is intuited and offered as a better way of understanding things. A new paradigm is appearing.

Kuhn argues that the appearance of a new scientific paradigm qualifies as an event with truly revolutionary implications.

> *New theories cannot arise without destructive changes in the old beliefs about nature. A really new and radical theory is never just an addition or increment to the existing knowledge. It changes basic rules, requires drastic revision or reformulation of the fundamental assumptions of prior theory, and involves re-evaluation of the existing facts and observations.* [4]

As examples, Kuhn mentions the shifts from Aristotelian to Newtonian physics, followed by another from Newtonian to Einsteinian quantum physics; from the Ptolemaic geocentric system to the astronomy of Copernicus and Galileo; from phlogiston theory to Lavoisier's oxygen chemistry. Each of these obligated a rejection of time-honored and widely accepted ways of viewing the world in favor of alternatives that were considered, in the beginning, to be incompatible or impossible. Some paradigm shifts are limited to specific fields of knowledge, while others can have a sweeping influence in a number of disciplines.

Paradigm Competence

It is important to understand that even though a new paradigm may seem to supersede or replace a previous one, it is not appropriate to classify the older as "wrong" and the newer as "right." In their time and place, each offers important and practical insights as to how events and objects "should" be treated. Each is useful, within a given context and when faced with certain circumstances. When one is considering a new way of looking at things, an old metaphor cautions, *"Don't cast out the baby with the bath."* This admonition may be especially important for managers, who are often encouraged to adopt the "latest and best" management consultant's theories.

The manager who is *paradigm competent,* who possesses knowledge of a variety of conceptual frameworks, will be able to make judgments as to the applicability and worth of different ways of seeing things, of approaching and analyzing problems. He will not be a prisoner of a single paradigm. In some contexts, and with some people, the "older" paradigm may yield good results. But if it is not working, and problems are not responding to that way of looking at things, then clearly it is time to test the usefulness of an alternative approach.

Why Are Paradigms Important?

Any thoughtful person is interested in the accuracy or "truthfulness" of his knowledge in relation to what he or she perceives as "reality." Knowledge that does not conform to reality is recognized to be of limited use, and may lead people to act in innocent but grievous error. This is particularly true for managers, who have the responsibility of directing the work of others.

---

4.   In Grof, *Beyond the Brain.* p. 6

Deriving "true" knowledge, however, is a very complex problem. It has been the highest objective of scientists and philosophers since it was recognized by the early Greeks that there is a significant difference between *appearances,* as they are presented to the observer, and *essences,* which refer to unchanging qualities of objects that characterize its "true" being, however appearances might vary. The history of Greek philosophy reveals that by the time of Plato, they had already decided that the path to true knowledge (they called it *episteme*) lay in the search for, and discovery of the changeless, *essential* qualities of things. Appearances can be deceptive; essences are enduring.

What remained unexamined for centuries was the critical importance of background assumptions about the nature of things that are incorporated into a thing's naming, or definition. Until Immanuel Kant's *Critique of Pure Reason* appeared in 1787, there was a centuries old, naive belief in the scientific community that true knowledge (*episteme*) consisted of a faithful copy in the mind of objective phenomena external to the observer.

Cassirer calls this the *copy theory* of knowledge, and he points out why, since Kant, the centuries old "copy theory" of knowledge had to be abandoned. For Kant introduced irrefutable evidence of *a priori* processing in the mind which necessarily must take place prior to the mind's actual perceptive recognition of what it is seeing. Cassirer affirms the *a priori* importance of how the mind participates in the formation of *all* knowledge:

> *The transformation is as momentous as a Copernican revolution, a wholly new orientation toward the problem of knowledge. It is the hypothesis that, instead of human knowledge being shaped to reality, it is our human judgment which determines whatever is to have the character of being reality for us. The roles are reversed—the judgment conditions reality.*[5]

Kant had given himself to examining what the mind knows, or can know, without any input from our five senses. Kant used the term *"pure"* reason to refer to mental activity unsullied by any sensations, that is, prior to, *a priori,* to sensory input. His question was, Is there *a priori* knowledge? Does the mind have any *a priori* programming affecting the interpretation of sensory information? Is there any knowledge that does not originate in the world external to our five senses, as was then affirmed by empiricists such as John Locke?

---

5.   In Ernst Cassirer, *Phenomenology of Symbolic Forms, Volume One: Language.* Translated by Ralph Manheim from *Philosophie der symbolischen Formen: Die Sprache,* (1923). (New Haven: Yale University Press, 1955) p. 6

Kant cited mathematical reasoning as a first example. He was able to show that mathematical logic exists without any reference at all to external sensation, because "eight and five are thirteen" without any reference whatever to external objects or the sensory perception of them. He went on to show that the human mind is pre-programmed to process sensory information in predetermined ways. In other words, it is impossible for us to perceive anything at all without the mind having made anticipatory judgments, in the very act of perceiving, as to what this *is* that I am observing. One cannot trust any longer that our senses can provide us with a true picture of the physical reality out there. Our own judgments are constantly conditioning, indeed, they are *creating* for us, the reality we naively believe we are observing. Cassirer declares unequivocally why it is necessary to study and understand knowledge paradigms in use, because they have been incorporated unconsciously into our every idea:

> *Since man is involved in the knowing, his doing so has part in the resultant knowledge and so there can be no pure transcript of the truth in either sense or reason. We must study the knowing before we can claim knowledge of something beyond it called ultimate reality.*[6]

The pre-Kantian, empiricist view of the human mind as a passive processor of simple ideas had been the guarantee, from Aristotle until Kant, that a scientist could trust his reasoned observations to deliver a faithful copy of the reality he was studying. A century after the Kantian revolution, Edmund Husserl, creator of the philosophy called phenomenology, illustrated from a different perspective how the mind is *actively* engaged in every perception which humans have. Husserl introduced the term ***intentionality*** to illustrate his belief that man can perceive something only as he ***intends*** to perceive it—that is, by conforming the stream of primary sensory data into some pattern that is recognizable. To dramatize this with an illustration, Husserl writes that in the process of perception, a man *"fires his intentionality at the object being perceived much like a man fires a gun."*[7]

---

6.   Ernst Cassirer, *The Phenomenology of Symbolic Forms.* (New Haven: Yale University Press, 1955). *VOL. I, Language.* p.3

7.   In Colin Wilson, *Introduction to the New Existentialism.* (London: Hutchinson & Company, Ltd., 1966) p.59. See also Joseph J. Kockelmans, *Phenomenology and Physical Science.* (Pittsburgh, Duquesne University Press, 1966) p.8, *et seq.*, and Pierre Thevenaz, *What is Phenomenology?* (Chicago: Quadrangle Books, 1962) pp. 18, 48, *et seq.*

Unexamined Paradigm Assumptions

The study of paradigms is vitally important because the dominant paradigms we have learned from our culture, that is, the complex of assumptions and values which create "reality" for us, are pre-judging, and pre-determining our every perception of what is going on. Lest we remain prisoners of one or another of these cultural paradigms, and thereby blinded to alternative ways of seeing things, we need to call up for review the mostly unexamined assumptions that have created and also limit this that we call "reality." A "paradigm shift" is another name for a modification of these assumptions.

Four Exemplar Paradigms

In the chapters that follow, we intend to describe and illustrate with some examples, how differing assumptions about the world, about people, and about knowledge of reality can create alternative conceptual paradigms. We begin with a description of the most common knowledge framework utilized in Western cultures, called the **"positive science"** paradigm. We next explore the important modifications to conceptualizations of physical reality introduced in this century by the study of atomic phenomena and the emergence of **quantum physics.** In the section that follows, we review oriental **mysticism** and the experience of the paradoxical as useful, and sometimes necessary, ways to interpret the universe. By the way, both of these are strongly supported by our intuitive capabilities. We conclude with a sketch of how **existential** authors conceptualize the world of human existence, and how this alternative framework can be of assistance to managers.

Chapter 2:
The Positive Science Paradigm

Newtonian-Cartesian science has created a very negative image of human beings, depicting them as biological machines driven by instinctual impulses of a bestial nature. It has no genuine recognition of higher values, such as spiritual awareness, feelings of love, aesthetic needs, or sense of justice.... This image endorses individualism, egoistic emphasis, competition, and the principle of "survival of the fittest" as natural and essentially healthy tendencies.

—Stanislav Grof, *Beyond the Brain.* NY: SUNY, 1985.

What you will find in this chapter

1. **The Positive Science paradigm and its vision of the world**

2. **Positive science; its evolution**

3. **John Locke's psychology; the "tabula rasa" view**

4. **The need for alternative paradigms**

Not many are aware that the pervasive ideas characterizing western views of the natural world were codified by Aristotle more than two millennia ago, and subsequently elaborated by philosophers of the Middle Ages. The Aristotelian world view, fixed in tradition, became the philosophical base for a generally shared conception of a finite, mechanistic, purposefully ordered universe in which everything has its proper place. As elaborated by Aristotle and his successors, the "laws of nature" were considered to reflect a divine, cosmic, created order, describing regularities in the physical world. Of the post-Greek period, Fritjof Capra writes:

The notion of fundamental laws of nature was derived from the belief in a divine lawgiver which was deeply rooted in the Judeo-Christian tradition. In the words of Thomas Aquinas: "There is a certain Eternal Law, to wit, Reason, existing in the mind of God and governing the whole universe." The notion of an eternal, divine law of nature greatly influenced Western philosophy and science. To discover the ultimate fundamental laws of nature remained the aim of natural scientists for three centuries following Newton.[1]

The conceptualization of a mechanistic, ordered, universe was central to the Greek understanding of the nature of knowledge, since the goal of inquiry was to discover the *essential* nature of objects or concepts. They searched for an *essence*, which persisted in the shadows, behind the surface appearance of objects, as they appeared to the viewer. This *essential nature* was bound up in the laws of cause and effect thought to govern the whole of physical nature. In his *Analytica Posteriora,* Aristotle writes:

...now to know its essential nature is, as we said, the same as to know the cause of a thing's existence, and the proof of this depends on the fact that a thing must have a cause.[2]
...we suppose ourselves to possess unqualified scientific knowledge of a thing, as opposed to knowing it in the accidental way in which the sophist knows, when we think that we know the cause on which the fact depends, as the cause of that fact and of no other, and, further, that fact could not be other than it is.[3]

To "know" something was to understand its *essence*, and to know its essence depended upon understanding its *necessary cause*, i.e., what event or force *caused* it to be what it was. The assumption was that this universe was mechanistically law-like and ordered, otherwise causal relationships could not exist.

The idea of a mechanistic, cause-effect ordered universe has a long history. Capra points out that 2,500 years ago, at the beginnings of the recorded history of the study of physics, there occurred a philosophical disagreement in Greece about the nature of the world, one which had momentous implications for the later course of Western science.

1.   Fritjof Capra, *The Tao of Physics: An Exploration of the Parallels Between Modern Physics and Eastern Mysticism.* (Boulder, Colorado: Shambhala Publications, Inc. 1975) p. 287
2.   See *Analytica Posteriora.* Book II:8, in W. E. Ross, ed., *The Works of Aristotle.* (Oxford, 1928)
3.   Ross, *Op.cit., Analytica Posteriora.* Book I:2

The roots of physics, as of all Western science, are to be found in the first period of Greek philosophy in the sixth century BC, in a culture where science, philosophy, and religion were not separated. The sages of the Milesian school in Ionia were not concerned with such distinctions. Their aim was to discover the essential nature, or real constitution, of things which they called 'physis.' The term 'physics' is derived from this Greek word and meant therefore, originally, the endeavor of seeing the essential nature of things.[4]

The organic view of the Milesians actually was very close to that of ancient Indian and Chinese philosophy. Even stronger parallels to Eastern thought, however, are found in the philosophy of Heraclitus of Ephesus, who believed in a world of perpetual change, of eternal 'Becoming.' For Heraclitus, all ideas of *static* being were based on deception. He taught that constant changes in the world arise from the dynamic and cyclic interplay of opposites, and he saw any pair of opposites as a unity.[5]

The break with the views of Heraclitus of Ephesus concerning whether or not the world that we perceive is, or is not, in a condition of constant flux or change arose from Parmenides of Elea, who strongly opposed the world view of Heraclitus.

[Parmenides] considered change to be impossible and regarded the changes we seem to perceive in the world as mere illusions of the senses. The concept of the indestructible substance as the subject of varying properties grew out of this philosophy and became one of the fundamental concepts of Western thought.[6]

Thus, the destiny of Western science and civilization was determined when Greek philosophy ultimately preferred the world view of Parmenides over that of Heraclitus. As a result, Western science developed around a world view emphasizing a stable reality in which true knowledge depends upon understanding unchanging essences of objects in the physical universe. Parmenides assumed that a Divine Principle stands above all gods and men, a belief that led ultimately to the separation of spirit and matter and to the dualism that became characteristic of Western philosophy and the Judeo-Christian religion.

---

4.   Capra, *The Tao of Physics*. p. 20
5.   Capra, *The Tao of Physics*. p. 20
6.   Capra, *The Tao of Physics*, p. 21

Knowledge of the World

Two basic elements characterized Aristotle's understanding of the relationship between knowledge and objects in the physical world. The first was that the image or perception in the mind was, or could be, identical with, or a true copy of, the object that was being perceived. In his ***Psychology,*** he writes:

> *Actual knowledge is identical with the known object.... what obviously occurs is that a sense faculty which is already potentially sentient is made actively sentient by the presence of a sensible object, without being thereby affected or qualitatively altered...*[7]

The second element characterizing the Aristotelian description of knowledge was that *true,* or *scientific* knowledge (*episteme*) did not result from naive perceptions, but was a product of the rational processing of perceptions by the mind, as could be formalized in the syllogism. Aristotle divided reasoning into two forms: *inductive* and *syllogistic.* Induction was the name he gave to the process of abstracting generalizations or universals from observed reality, while the syllogism was the name he gave to a form of logical reasoning which is at the base of the Aristotelian system of logic. In *Analytica Posteriora*, he writes:

> *Scientific knowledge is not possible through the act of perception.... scientific knowledge involves the recognition of the commensurate universal...The commensurate universal is precious because it makes clear the cause; so that in case of facts like these which have a cause other than themselves, the universal is more precious than sense perception and intuition.*[8]

In Aristotle's scheme of things, induction was the name of the process by which an observer intuited certain "commensurate universals," generalizations about the essences of things. These were then formally proposed as premises upon which the syllogistic or logical/rational reasoning proceeded, and by which one eventually derived certain knowledge or *truth (episteme).* Thus, learning and teaching utilized both modes, proceeding sometimes by induction and sometimes by the syllogism.[9]

---

7. See *Psychology. Book III:7,* in Philip Wheelwrite, (Trans.) ***Aristotle.*** (NY: The Odyssey Press, 1951). p.149
8. Ross, *Op.cit.,* Analytica Posteriora. Book I:31
9. Wheelwrite, *Op.cit.,* Nichomachean Ethics. Book VI:3

One additional quality needs to be pointed out about the Aristotelian knowledge system: it was completely mechanistic—it was based on a machine-like universe which was unitary, which sprang from a First Cause, from which all subsequent cause-and-effect relationships emanated, each in its proper hierarchical relationship to the other. And, since knowledge of the world was held to be in every way identical to the physical world itself, true knowledge was thought to be a faithful copy of the world itself.

Descartes, Comte, and Positive Science

The Aristotelian method, emphasizing syllogistic or logical reasoning, gave rise to the scholasticism of the Middle Ages, during which devoted practitioners of science seemed to minimize actual observation of the physical world in their pursuit of "scientific" knowledge. In the twelfth and thirteenth centuries, however, important advances began to be made in astronomy and in other physical sciences that engaged in a more detailed examination of the physical world itself.

The work of the famous French mathematician and philosopher, René Descartes, seems to mark the beginning of an important shift in the thinking of the scientific community of Europe concerning the relationship between men, objects, and knowledge. Building upon traditionally held "natural law" ideas, to the effect that the world and the universe are basically ordered constructions responding to inviolable laws which regulate the entire cosmos, and upon recent advances in the field of mathematics, Descartes wanted to create a universal scientific language system, based upon mathematics, which would enable man both to investigate as well as to communicate a growing knowledge about this ordered cosmos.[10]

The Evolution of Positive Science

Flushed with the palpable success of the development of the physical sciences in the mid-1800s, Auguste Comte, with his fellow *Encyclopedists*, systematized the emerging Newtonian-Cartesian "scientific" paradigm and gave it its **"positive science"** name. He taught that since the beginnings of Western civilization, each new system of knowledge has necessarily progressed through three stages: The

---

10. For a useful review of the historical development of these ideas, see William A. Luijpen and Henry J. Koren, **A** *First Introduction to Existential Phenomenology*. (Pittsburgh, Pa: Duquesne University Press, 1969) pp.28-74

first was the **mythical or religious stage,** in which man understands the phenomena under investigation with the help of mythical or religious conceptualizations to explain otherwise incomprehensible factors. The second was the **metaphysical stage**, in which some of the purely mythical aspects begin to give way to more specific knowledge about physical phenomena being observed. The third, and final stage was the **"positive science" stage,** in which there is no longer any need of invoking mythical or metaphysical factors to explain the physical phenomena under investigation—its entirely physical characteristics and functions were now thought to be "objectively" understood, to be controllable, and predictable.

Following Newton, Descartes, and Comte most European scientists turned their attention away from Aristotle's syllogistic analysis of man's relationships to the physical world in favor of the emerging "positive science" emphasis on the analysis of the physical objects themselves. In contrast to the Aristotelian emphasis upon a search for essences or universals, derived by means of syllogistic reasoning, the emerging positive science paradigm turned away from emphasis on mental faculties to a meticulous and detailed examination of physical objects themselves.

No longer could the scientist be content with an inductive analysis of as many particularistic instances as one could conveniently observe; a new and "scientific" methodology emerged, focused on the object, using a "laboratory method" whereby evidence or proof was deduced from observations of the phenomena themselves. Truth became an empirical thing, located in the external world of objects. It did not make any difference which experimenter set in motion the sequence of events—when law-like, causal relationships between events were established by observation of the phenomena themselves, then one had arrived a "positive science" proof, a truth based upon purely physical evidence observable by the five senses.

Lockean Psychology

Coincidentally with the emerging positive science paradigm, John Locke presented a modified version of the thinking mind which was extraordinarily compatible with the new emphasis on the physical analysis of objects, and which gave great authenticity and power to the positive science schema advocated by Comte. Briefly, Locke postulated that man's mind functions like a *"tabula rasa;"* a kind of "blank slate" upon which the five sensory streams project their impressions derived from object world stimuli.[11]

This view of the functioning mind seemed to confirm the emerging definition of truth, evidence, meaning, etc., as being legitimately located in the external world of objects. For, if man's mind was only the passive recorder of sensory impressions which emanated from the objects under examination, then proof, evidence, and ultimately, truth, resided in the world exterior to man. His mind was nothing more than a passive processor of stimuli that had their source, without exception, in the external physical world.

Our contemporary concern with "hard" facts, with empirical data, with "positive proof," with the "substance" of the matter, all have their roots in the positive science paradigm and the Lockean explanation of the functioning mind as a passive recorder of sensory impressions originating in the object or physical world and transmitted to the "tabula rasa" mind by means of the five senses. It is based upon an Aristotelian notion that knowledge of an object can be identical with the object itself.

It must be recognized that this positive science paradigm has yielded unparalleled knowledge of the physical world, and unparalleled control over it, to Western civilization. The "scientific method" has proven to be extraordinarily successful in dealing with the world of physical objects. Unfortunately, humans refuse to be categorized as equivalent to physical objects.

We have described two phases in a basically Aristotelian knowledge system commonly taught and utilized in the Western world as our culture has attempted to cope with "reality," organizational and/or other. This positive science system, employing compatible philosophical and psychological metaphors, in a first stage placed emphasis on the logical processing of induced premises within the mind of the observer or scholar. In a second, or positive science stage, proof, truth, and evidence were externalized, that is, were seen as being located in external objects themselves rather than being products of the mind.[12] This gave great emphasis and great power in dealing with the object world by means of the scientific method. But at the same time it distorted a full understanding of the meaning of human existence by treating persons as "objects" to be analyzed by the same "scientific" methods used to analyze other physical objects and interactions.

---

11.   While Locke is generally credited with the original description of the functioning mind as a "tabula rasa," the same idea is found in Aristotle's psychology. Aristotle writes, "what it (mind) thinks must be in it just as characters may be said to be on a writing tablet on which as yet nothing actually stands written: this is exactly what happens with mind." in *De Anima, Book III:4*

The Need for Alternative Paradigms

By the beginning of the 20th Century, two themes of inquiry emerging from quite different sources began to question the hegemony of the positive science paradigm in Western civilization. The first, springing from criticisms of religious, social and political thought in Europe, launched a rebellion against the unitary, mechanistic, objective view of the world as being inappropriate for the study of how people perceive their existence and make choices that affect their lives. The work of a number of disparate writers, it eventually came to be called **existentialism**.

The second, born out of research into electromagnetic phenomena, atomic physics, and questioning about the commonly held perceptions of space, time, and energy, gave rise to evidence that the Newtonian-positive science views of the physical world no longer served to explain the new discoveries. In 1905, Albert Einstein proposed his "Special Theory of Relativity" which overturned centuries-old conceptualizations of the most basic elements of the physical universe. Continuing research into the makeup of the atom gave rise to discoveries in particle physics, and the evolution of **quantum theory** to explain events observed in the new research efforts.

Existentialism questioned age-old assumptions about a mechanistic, ordered, and predictable universe from the point of view of the humans attempting to give meaning to their existence. Quantum theory disproved most of the commonly held assumptions about the basic building blocks of the physical universe. Neither could any longer support the root assumptions about a cause/effect related physical world which formed the basis of the familiar positive science paradigm which had been such an important part of Western science and culture. Both existentialism and quantum physics cried out for alternative paradigms to provide a framework within which to understand and explain elements which were the focus of their studies.

---

12.   Jean Piaget demonstrates the naive attractiveness of the notion that proof or evidence emerges naturally from the data itself, by describing its appearance in children at about the age of seven years. "The point of this illustration is that the older child takes as self-evident, or *a priori,* what only a few short years ago he didn't know existed! Once a concept is constructed, it is immediately *externalized* so that it appears to the subject as a perceptually given property of the object and independent of the subject's own mental activity." Jean Piaget, *Six Psychological Studies.* (NY: Random House, 1967) p. xii.

Kuhn, and other observers of the evolution of knowledge frameworks, recognize that people are reluctant to abandon a preferred way of looking at things, especially when that point of view has usually been successful. Furthermore, learning to "see" a world stitched together based on new and different principles can involve a radical and tortuous giving up of cherished teachings and deeply held values. In some cases, a paradigm change is radical and deep enough to be considered a kind of "new birth" in which nearly every element in one's reality is seen with new eyes, forever after.

However, we are here advocating a kind of **paradigm competence**, in which the manager learns how to change his conceptual perspective in order to enable the intuitive faculties of his mind to "see" the problem from several different perspectives, and to be able to invent newly creative solutions. To that end, we propose to describe some old and new alternatives to the familiar positive science paradigm in the sections that follow.

Chapter 3:
The Quantum Physics Paradigm

Although for the practical purposes of daily life one still thinks in terms of solid matter, three-dimensional space, unidirectional time, and linear causality, the philosophical understanding of existence becomes much more complex and sophisticated; it approaches that found in the great mystical traditions of the world.

—Stanislav Grof, *Beyond the Brain. NY: SUNY, 1985*

What you will find in this chapter

1. **A more sophisticated paradigm**

2. **Divergent Western and Eastern philosophies**

3. **Limitations of cause-effect explanations**

4. **Perceptions and consciousness: Intentional?**

5. **What is meant by "valid knowledge"?**

Since the turn of the century, there has been a conceptual and scientific revolution in the field of physics, a revolution that has wide-ranging and sometimes unexpected implications as concerns the potential for a new and deeper understanding of relationships between humans and the universe in which we live. Developments in the field of particle physics have completely displaced the familiar views of Newton concerning the atomic nature of physical objects and earlier cause-effect explanations of a mechanistic universe. Not only has understanding of the physical world been radically modified, but along with them notions explaining the functioning of the human mind and its possibilities of transcending limitations imposed by the traditional scientific views of what constitutes empirical proof and evidence.

This section reviews the radical changes in the paradigm of western "positive science" brought about by discoveries since 1900 relating to the nature and composition of the atom, and leading to the emergence of "quantum" theory, based upon Einstein's "special theory of relativity," first published in 1905. A deeper understanding of the many sub-atomic particles making up what used to be considered the basic building blocks of all "solid" material in the universe has worked a radical, paradigmatic revolution in our traditional ideas of such fundamental categories as space and time, and of our ability to understand and know the "essential" nature of physical objects in the world.

Much of the material in this section is drawn from the work of Fritjof Capra in *The Tao of Physics,*[1] a comprehensive review of how research in particle physics has radically modified our conceptions of the nature of matter. Capra and other physicists, finding it necessary to search beyond the Greek-originated, Newtonian-Cartesian view of physical matter, came to learn that Eastern philosophies have long dealt with some of the counter-intuitive paradoxes discovered in quantum descriptions of atomic phenomena.

Based upon what is now known, it appears impossible for the human mind to "picture" conceptually a four-dimensioned cosmos in which time is non-linear, space is curved by gravitational forces, energy and mass are interchangeable, and light may be viewed usefully as being constituted by both particles and waves. Given this frustrating impossibility, what options are available to us? It turns out that Eastern mystical philosophies have long perceived the world as a non-objective and paradoxically unified cosmos. They believe that humans can have direct knowledge of this universe through an experientially oriented, meditative mode. Faced with the relativistic paradoxes which emerge from quantum physics, the Eastern modes of understanding seem to offer some conceptual advantages over traditional western views of a differentiated, categorized, fragmented physical universe.

Divergent Western and Eastern Philosophies

Western and Eastern philosophies diverged 2,500 years ago when the Greeks chose the Eleatic school of Parmenides, which held perceptions of change to be mere illusions of our senses, over the views of Heraclitus, who taught that the

---

1.   Fritjof Capra, *The Tao of Physics: An Exploration of the Parallels Between Modern Physics and Eastern Mysticism.* (Boulder, Colorado: Shambhala Publications, Inc. 1975)

entire universe is in a constant state of flux. Parmenides taught that to know something truly was to understand the *essence* of it, those qualities that did *not* change even when its appearances changed.

In contrast to the Greek focus on static "essences," Eastern philosophies developed separately from, but similar to, the views Heraclitus held about the cosmos, that is, by conceptualizing the universe as being constantly in flux. When everything is constantly changing, nothing can be perceived as concrete, or unchanging, but capturing such conditions with a suitable conceptual paradigm proves to be a challenge, especially for Western-trained scientists.[2]

The Eastern mystics repeatedly insist that an ultimate reality can never be realized as an object of reasoning or of "demonstrable" knowledge. It can never be described adequately in words, because it lies beyond the realms of the senses and of the intellect from which words and concepts are derived. "Absolute" knowledge is thus an entirely non-intellectual experience of reality, an experience which the mystics believe arises out of a non-ordinary state of consciousness which they call a "meditative" or mystical state. There is abundant reference to such states in the testimony of numerous mystics from East and West, and the renowned American psychologist, William James, wrote:

> *Our normal waking consciousness, rational consciousness, as we call it, is but one special type of consciousness, whilst all about it, parted from it by the filmiest of screens, there lie potential forms of consciousness entirely different.*[3]

Although physicists are mainly concerned with rational knowledge and mystics with intuitive knowledge, both types of knowledge occur in both fields. For example, both Hindu Vedanta and Buddhist Madhyamika are highly intellectual schools. On the other hand, the Taoists have always had a deep mistrust of reason and logic, and Zen, which grew out of Buddhism but was strongly influenced by Taoism, prides itself on being "without words, without explanations, without

---

2.   Alfred North Whitehead is a singular example of a Western-trained philosopher who attempted to build a coherent philosophy around the idea of a world in constant flux. His philosophical writings spanned the two decades of the 1920s and 1930s in England and the United States. His categorical scheme for "process philosophy" is outlined in *Process and Reality* (NY: Macmillan, Free Press, 1969) pp. 22-35

3.   William James, *The Varieties of Religious Experience*. (NY: Longmans, Green & Co., 1935) p.388

instructions, without knowledge."[4] A well-known Zen phrase says, "The instant you speak about a thing you miss the mark."

The Positive Science "Zone of Middle Dimensions"

For positive science, the Newtonian-Cartesian model of the physical world seemed adequate and highly successful, as long as physicists were exploring phenomena of everyday experience, sometimes called "the zone of middle dimensions," that is, neither the interior of atoms nor the birth of stars. Nevertheless, Grof observes:

> *Once they started making excursions beyond the limits of ordinary perception into the microworld of subatomic processes and into the macroworld of astrophysics, the Newtonian-Cartesian model became untenable and had to be transcended.*[5]

Capra recounts that the revolutionary changes in the study of physics began in the nineteenth century with the experiments of Faraday and Maxwell on electromagnetic phenomena. Their experimental work led them to the creation of the idea of a "force field" to explain phenomena associated with electromagnetism. Their conceptualization of a force field came to displace the Newtonian concept of mechanical force, because magnetic force fields can be studied with no reference to physical bodies. Furthermore, it led to the discovery that light is a rapidly alternating electromagnetic field traveling through space in the form of waves. Eventually a comprehensive theory of electromagnetism based on this discovery made it possible to relate all wave phenomena, from low frequency radio waves to cosmic rays, to differences in frequency of oscillation. At first, these electromagnetic waves were conceived as vibrations of a very light, space-filling substance called "ether" in accordance with Newtonian paradigm. However, a famous experiment by Michelson and Morley proved that Newton's "ether" does not exist.

Thus, the first decades of the twentieth century introduced unexpected developments in physics that revolutionized the Aristotelian-Newtonian model of the universe. In 1905 Albert Einstein published two papers which introduced what came to be called the quantum theory of atomic phenomena. In the first paper he formulated the principles of his *special theory of relativity,* and in the second he suggested a new way of looking at light that was later elaborated into the *quantum theory* of atomic processes.

---

4.   Capra, *The Tao of Physics*. p. 34
5.   Grof, *Beyond the Brain,* p. 52

Einstein's theory of relativity was an absolutely radical departure from Newtonian models of the physical world.

> *The theory of relativity and the new atomic theory undermined all the basic concepts of Newtonian physics: the existence of absolute time and space, the solid material nature of the universe, the definition of physical forces, the strictly deterministic system of explanation, and the ideal of objective description of phenomena without including the observer.*[6]

Non-Standard Time and Space

According to the theory of relativity, space is not three-dimensional and time is not linear. Space and time cannot be considered separate entities; rather, they are interwoven, one with the other, forming a four-dimensional continuum called "space-time." Contrary to the Aristotelian-Newtonian model of the world, the flow of time is not uniform; it rather depends upon where the observers are and their relative velocities with respect to the event being observed. It appears that massive objects can bend rays of light, and variations in the field of gravity in different parts of the universe have a curving effect on space that makes time flow at different rates.

As for the idea of solid matter made up of atoms, the discovery of x-rays and radioactive elements led to further experiments that reveal that atoms are not hard and solid units of matter, but consist of vast spaces in which small particles, called electrons, revolve around a nucleus. The study of these atomic processes presented scientists with some strange paradoxes that arise when attempting to explain the new findings in the framework of traditional physics. As Einstein had predicted, mass and energy are transmutable. And quantum physics demonstrated that subatomic particles had characteristics that showed a paradoxically dual nature. Depending upon the arrangement of the experiment, they sometimes appeared as particles, and other times as waves. A similar ambiguity appears in the nature of light, which, in some experiments, shows the properties of an electromagnetic field, and in others seems to be made up of distinct energy quanta, called photons, which are massless and travel with the speed of light.

---

6.   In Grof, *Beyond the Brain*, p. 53

Quantum Paradoxes of Logic

Aristotelian syllogistic logic was based on the idea that something either *is* or it *is not*; light must be *either* a particle or a wave. Evidence demonstrating that light is both waves and particles clearly violates the ground rules of traditional logic. The image of a particle implies an entity confined to a small volume or a finite region of space, whereas the idea of a wave is diffuse and spread over wide regions of space. In quantum physics, these two states are logically exclusive one of the other, yet both are equally necessary for a comprehensive understanding of the phenomena.

Cause-Effect Explanations Useless

Another paradigm problem presents itself in the domain of the quantum, where the concept of *causality* is useless, and the idea of obtaining an *objectively true picture* of physical reality is out of the question. For man, searching for true knowledge of the world, there is no longer anything solid from whence to begin. The hope of obtaining an objective truth of how things "really" are has had to be abandoned with the recognition that the positive science paradigm which imagined this to be possible had to be consigned to the trash bin of the history of ideas.

Thus, since the beginning of this century, virtually everything thought to be solid and stable about the physical universe has turned out to be a myth. The Newtonian model of solid material bodies moving with Euclidean characteristics in geometric space is now recognized as generally invalid except in the "zone of middle dimensions," where it continues to be commonly employed in the realm of everyday experience.

Copy vs. Symbolic Theories of Knowledge

All theories of natural phenomena, including natural laws, are now recognized to be creations of the human mind, and products of the culture in which they appear. The major philosopher dealing with the epistemological issues of the relation between what we believe we know and what is actually "out there," exterior to our skin, is the neo-Kantian, Ernst Cassirer. Recognizing that the "copy theory" of knowledge had to be abandoned after Kant demonstrated the mind does not, indeed *cannot*, stamp a true picture of objective reality on the memory by means of the senses, Cassirer developed an alternative "symbolic theory" of knowledge, which has come to displace the naive "copy" theory.

All knowledge is held to be man's own symbolic creation, his very personal, internal representations of what he believes his senses are telling him. The culture in which he is formed plays an extremely important role in teaching him what is important and useful as knowledge, and colors every judgment as to what is being perceived and what the perception means.

The Idea of Intentional Perceptions

Edmund Husserl, developer of the field of phenomenology, labeled this process "intentionality." In a pre-conscious stage of perception, the mind seems to search for recognizable patterns in the five sensory data streams, patterns which are then matched with others previously memorized from earlier cultural experiences and training. When a match is made, there is "recognition" at some level of pre-consciousness. Having identified what is happening, now the intentional mind can interpret it, and choose an appropriate response. Thus, there is "intentionality" in every act of recognition—having recognized what the sensory streams relate to, the mind interprets what it means, and what, if any, action should be taken in that cultural context.

Consciousness Itself Is Intentional

The mystery of the phenomena we call "consciousness" is a topic of current concern to the medical profession, as well as to psychologists and philosophers. The idea of consciousness being largely "illusion" is too much for many conservative philosophers, who prefer to assign explanations of consciousness to electro-chemical operations and the inter-connectedness of neuron synapses in the brain. For example, Roger Penrose, University of Oxford mathematician, has argued that thought depends upon effects explicable only by quantum physics.[7]

Penrose represents the typical materialistic approach, which is to consider consciousness to be the product of innumerable physiological processes of a completely physical nature occurring in the brain. There are other philosophers and psychologists, however, who doubt that molecular explanations of mental functions will ever achieve an understanding of the full range of consciousness.

One innovative thinker on this subject, philosopher Daniel Dennett, Director of the Center for Cognitive Studies, Massachusetts Institute of Technology (MIT), is developing the idea that what we call "consciousness" is the product of

---

7.   *Scientific American*, (February, '96) p. 35

a "virtual machine" running in the brain. His declared intent has been to demystify the mind, "to bring philosophy up to date with biology." He also believes, like William James, that there are no clear boundaries between sensory inputs in consciousness, and other information of which we are only unconsciously aware. He observes that in fact, we are not conscious of anything at precisely the time we imagine. Our awareness is generated a little after the sensory perceptions have reached the brain, and have been interpreted as to their meaning.

Dennett holds that the key to understanding behavior, human and other, is to adopt an "intentional stance," i.e., to assume that the other is intending something in actions that are taken. Acting with intention has far-reaching implications, however, for it assumes beliefs and desires as the basis for the intention. Dennett views beliefs as "virtual" properties of brains, similar to software in a computer. Applying the intentional stance to humans led Dennett to his theory of consciousness.

> *Dennett's explanation is that at any instant there is no dividing line between sensory data that people are conscious of and those that are unconscious. In fact, we are not conscious of anything at precisely the time we imagine. What we experience, Dennett maintains, is generated a little after the fact, as the result of a competition among multiple patterns of mental activity propagating within the brain. Awareness comprises a small fraction of those mental events whose influence will persist and so alter beliefs about what just happened.*[8]

The Mind as a Video Camcorder

The modern video camera-recorder may be used as a metaphor for illustrating some of these ideas:

1. A camcorder records only what its lenses are looking at (i.e., what is intended)

2. Some lenses are telephoto, others wide angle; (some views are distant and narrowly focused, others wider, more general)

3. The magnetic recording on the camera's videotape is not a faithful copy of the reality the camera saw, but rather a magnetic representation of the video data.

---

8.   *Scientific American*, (February, '96) pp.34-35

4.   There may have been many interesting things happening simultaneously, but the camcorder captured only what the cameraman "intended."

The Problem of Valid Knowledge

If every act of perception is colored by one's personal intentionality, how then shall we test whether or not our view of reality is valid, or only personal? Cassirer teaches that there are many forms of valid knowledge, including language, myth, art, and religion. Valid knowledge is not limited to supposedly "scientific" teachings about the world of physical objects, but includes many other ways of "knowing" common to human cultures. There is evidence that the mind can "know" and use considerably more than what is provided to it by the five senses.

The epistemological problem facing the new paradigm is the overwhelming evidence that *all* forms of knowledge are colored by the point of view of the observer, and all communication of that knowledge is subject to conditionings introduced by the language employed. Thus, everything offered as evidence, proof, or validity, is meaningful only to the extent that there is *agreement on a shared frame of reference,* that is, on the paradigm in use.

Knowledge Paradigms and Communication

It is of recognized importance that managers should enjoy easy and effective communications with subordinates and superiors. This is yet another reason why managers need to be *paradigm competent.* When a person acquires the ability to perceive a scenario in several different ways, one becomes aware that different conceptual paradigms can change one's perception of reality, of what is going on, and what is being identified as the problem. Less-skilled subordinates may be doing their best to communicate their sense of what is needed to improve things, but unless the manager is aware of their view of the reality, it is possible to misunderstand or to misinterpret what is being reported.

All communications are encapsulated in a cultural and linguistic frame of reference. It is much easier to develop intuitive insights into a speaker's meaning if the manager can quickly sense the subordinate's way of looking at things. A paradigm-competent manager can direct a few questions aimed at "testing the reality" of the subordinate's perspective, and thereby rectify and clarify misunderstandings in communicating.

Chapter 4:
The Mystical World View

Strangely enough, management scholars may have greater tunnel vision than most because of their inordinate desire to be as scientific and legitimate as the so-called hard sciences. Of all the acts of management, the management of spirituality is one of the most important, mysterious, and frightening. And because of the nature of spirituality, ambivalence and fear are integral parts of this management.

—Ian I. Mitroff and Elizabeth Denton, *A Spiritual Audit of Corporate America.*

What you will find in this chapter

1. **The Usefulness of Intuitions**

2. **What should be understood by mysticism?**

3. **Intuition versus superstition**

4. **Tests for truth**

5. **The human versus materialistic views of the lived world**

The Usefulness of Intuitions

The mind surely is aware of much more than what is at the sharp focus of consciousness. When faced with the need to make decisions having many imponderables, managers must make use of intuitions in addition to available data. Eastern mysticism, with its different worldview and its teachings about the usefulness of meditation, employing training techniques that force learners to deal with paradox and ambiguity, becomes a source of ideas for how to add "reasoned intuition" to the manager's repertoire of useful skills.

It is increasingly evident that the complexity of visualizing a four-dimensioned, time and space relative, quantum-ordered cosmos eludes the conceptual capacities of the western mind, a mind acculturated to focus on a material world of "concrete" objects and facts resulting from physical measurements. Searching for experiential alternatives that might offer insights into the search for understanding of such complexities, a number of physicists have turned to Eastern mysticism as a possible arena of insight.

What Do We Mean By Mysticism?

In the context of this discussion, *mystical* can be defined as

> *"Having a meaning or reality that is neither apparent to the senses, nor obvious to the intelligence: based upon intuition, insight, or similar subjective experience; eluding efforts to explain or understand."*[1]

Capra explains that in Eastern traditions the mystical experience is described as a *direct insight that lies outside the realm of the intellect* and is obtained by watching rather than thinking; by looking inside oneself; by introspection. He goes on to point out that direct, intuitive insights are experienced by all of us in our everyday lives, and cites as examples the times when we are not able to recall the name of a person or place. Only after we have given up and shifted our attention to something else, suddenly, in a flash, we remember the forgotten name. Neither thinking nor reasoning is involved in this process. It is a sudden, immediate insight.[2]

When we must deal with ambiguity and paradoxical alternatives, the faculties of intuition and insight are indispensable, since logic and rationality will not resolve the paradoxes. The basic aim of Eastern mystic teaching is deliberately to silence the thinking mind in order to shift awareness from the rational to the intuitive mode of consciousness, in order to enhance the capability of the mind to function intuitively, to be able to "see" the wholeness of what seem to be contradictory but valued positions. Meditation is the most-used method for silencing the thinking mind. The Zen Buddhists use what might be thought of as a teach-

---

1.   Webster's *Third New International Dictionary*
2.   Capra, *The Tao of Physics.* p.34

ing technique designed deliberately to block rational thinking. Capra describes the teaching technique as follows:

> Koans *are carefully devised nonsensical riddles that are meant to make the student of Zen realize the limitations of logic and reasoning in a most dramatic way. The irrational wording and paradoxical content of these riddles makes it impossible to solve them by thinking. They are designed precisely to stop the thought processes and thus to make the student ready for the non-verbal experience of reality.*[3]

The Western-trained manager might well ask, "What possibly could be the benefit of learning to use the mind in a non-rational way?" We here argue that there are many times when a manager is faced with problems which must be resolved, but which include a) insufficient data, b) unpredictable outcomes, c) imponderable human factors, d) unknown or unpredictable political and market changes in the external environment. All of these unknowns make a thoroughly rational solution impossible, but yet decisions must be made.

The Meditative Approach to Understanding

The Eastern approach to this dilemma teaches one to try to grasp the entire reality of the situation by quieting the mind, and attempting to *experience* a unifying understanding of *all* of the conscious and unconscious capabilities of the mind. Some of the consciously available information can be processed by the rational mind, but at the margins of consciousness, the mind will also possess additional, non-conscious insights bearing on the problem. The manager trained in accessing these additional, non-rational, levels of the mind can be favored with insightful understanding of the ambiguous reality he is facing, and of how the problems might be creatively resolved.

Western and Eastern Uses of Intuition

The physical object emphasis characteristic of the positive science framework for centuries has disallowed intuition in favor of "empirical" proof, that is, physical evidence palpable to the five senses, and therefore located exterior to the observer. In effect, we have taught many generations to neither use nor trust "intuitions." Western culture has thus disallowed potential benefits from a "trained" subconscious, which is cultivated in Oriental cultures.

---

3.   Capra, *The Tao of Physics.* p.48

Western positive science has down-graded the mystical in favor of "objective" or rational approaches, while Eastern mysticism systematically trains people in methods to enhance the mind's use of perceptions at the margins of consciousness. The West has trained us systematically to disregard subconscious intuitions which might cross the mind, while the East entertains an assumption that the mind is aware of much more than what is at the forefront of consciousness, and this non-conscious awareness can be made available for our understanding in the form of intuitions.

Intuition vs. Superstition

Superstition *"A belief or practice resulting from ignorance, fear of the unknown, or trust in magic or chance."*[4]

Will the manager who wants to learn to trust his deepest intuitions fall prey to superstitious ignorance, fear of the unknown, chance, or magic? We want here to mark very clearly an important difference between *intuition* and *superstition,* since Western-educated scientists may be inclined to interpret any recommendation to include intuition as a valid part of decision-making as an invitation to abandon rationality in favor of superstition.

We believe that the intuitional faculties of the mind, those that help us to make use of data existing "at the margins of consciousness" and which aid us in grasping a larger view of a problem, can be enhanced by an Eastern mystical world view. However, the intuitional faculties we are advocating are far removed from any dependence upon superstitious beliefs in magic or chance as a basis for managerial choices or decisions. Consider the following important differences between *intuition* and *superstition:*

1. First and foremost, there is the matter of *knowledge.* The use of the faculties we call intuition are associated with as full or complete knowledge of the facts as are possible. Once filled with the facts, intuition can come into play to enhance the scope and quality of the decision. In contrast, superstition is associated with ignorance and fear: ignorance of the facts bearing on the problem, and fear of the unknown.

---

4.   Webster's Third New International Dictionary

2. Even when it is difficult or impossible to gather all the facts of the case, and even when there are many unknowns and imponderables, superstition yet has no legitimate place in the manager's decision-making, it is completely out of the question as a substitute for a healthy intuition. Superstition is *fear* of the unknown, leading to a blind and ungrounded turning to chance or to folk-magic. In contrast, intuition is accompanied by *optimism* and a sense of *confidence* in the outcome, rather than fear.

3. Intuition begins with a *rational* study of available facts, a *rational* consideration of known alternatives, and a *rational* assessment of potential risks associated with the imponderables. Having done this, if the decision is yet not clear, then it is time to turn to meditation, to free the mind to be able to "see" an intuitively best choice. The faculty of intuition becomes complementary to rational consideration, adding to it by permitting the meditative mind to incorporate other factors which lie at the margins of consciousness, unrecoverable and unusable to the focused and conscious rational processes.

One of the important historic victories in Western science was the struggle to free its practitioners from long-held superstitions, from trusting in "magic" and/ or chance rather than searching for rational-materialistic explanations for phenomena. It was especially vivid for Auguste Comte and his collaborators, as they battled the Roman Catholic Church over its claim to "absolute" or "revealed" truth which the propagators of the new "positive science" disdained and scorned as superstitious metaphysics.

In opposition to the idea of a truth which depends upon belief, religious or other, Comtean positive science developed a strong bias favoring a search for proof or truth which does not depend upon what an observer believes. Rather, the only evidence considered scientifically admissible has to come from visible or palpable material objects or events located external to the observer. This rule or method was thought to protect the search for truth from errors introduced by personal beliefs.

Kantian Tests for Truth

Within this framework, Immanuel Kant described two *"tests for truth"* which are commonly advocated in the rationalistic West. One he called the *correspondence theory* and the other the *coherence theory*. We use the correspondence theory to judge the truth of a statement when we use our five senses to test whether or not the statement, as we understand it, "corresponds" to what our senses tell us.

Someone declares that it is raining. We test whether or not this is true by attempting to gather a redundancy of information from our five senses: do we see, feel, or hear raindrops falling? does it smell like rain? is the ground wet? If the sensory evidence corresponds to the statement, we judge it to be true.

The coherence theory is a test of pure logic. The statement that "eight plus five make thirteen" is true with no external or sensory evidence whatsoever. It is true because in the *coherent* numerical system we use for arithmetic, the values of eight and five, when summed, can *only* yield thirteen. There is no other possible, correct answer.

When Correspondence and Coherence Theories Fail

These two tests are of inestimable value, as long as what is being tested is palpable to our senses or amenable to formal logic. But there are many, many real life experiences in which the circumstances do not fit so clearly into either of these two modes. For instance, how shall we test the truth of the statement, *"He loves her very much"*? He brings her flowers and perfume, and using the correspondence test, she has sensory evidence to believe that he truly loves her.

Sometime later, she comes to suspect that he is visiting another woman. Now, when he comes with flowers and perfume, will she judge that they are corresponding evidence of his true love, or an sly attempt to allay suspicion? This illustration reveals a third, vital element omitted in Kant's tests for truth: the element of *belief* and *intention.* Our intentional interpretation of sensory information includes internalized values about its importance and meaning, and these determine whether or not we choose to "believe" that it has a certain truth value. *Ultimately, then, truth depends upon what we choose to believe.* Centuries of Western efforts to define truth as residing in evidence exterior to the self have not erased the importance of beliefs and values in making judgments concerning the validity of the reality we create for ourselves.

Intuition: an Often-Used Judge of "Truth"

The authors believe that meditative introspection and intuitions can be a kind of guarantor that one's personal "truth" is indeed reality-based. If you think about it, we use faculties of intuition almost daily to detect sham, hypocrisy, or fraudulent intent on the part of persons we deal with. In other words, when we lack any clear, factual basis for making a judgment about a person's truthfulness, we regularly rely upon our intuitions to tell us about the truthfulness of the "reality" being represented. In a final analysis, intuition may well be the most reliable judge as to the validity of our own, as well as other, versions of "reality."

To summarize what has been covered thus far, we have described the main characteristics of two divergent and contrasting world views whose evolution we have traced for more than two millennia. European civilization and culture, following an ancient Greek choice to seek true knowledge in the static "essences" of material objects, chose to view the universe as mechanically ordered, hyperstable, relatively unchanging. The concrete knowledge they sought of this material world was focused on the unchanging essences of material objects, qualities which did not alter even though their visual appearances might change in different circumstances. Since Aristotle, the focus was on learning what forces or events "caused" something to be what it essentially was. This method of inquiry depends almost completely upon rational and intellectual faculties.

In contrast, Eastern culture preferred to view the universe as being in continual flux. They, too, recognized the error of naively believing things to be what they seemed to be, based upon their visual appearances. However, their method of learning to see "beyond" appearances, to discover an "ultimate reality" deeper than what things seemed to be, visually, came to be based upon insight and intuition rather than rationality. To enhance the mind's intuitional faculties, the better to "see" the unity and related wholeness of events in their lived world, they learned to practice quiet meditation, and various other techniques designed to consciously block the rational faculties in order to free a more creative, and more holistic faculty. *Table A* summarizes some of these features.

Table A: Summary Overview of Eastern and Western World Views

	Western, Materialistic World View	*Eastern, Mystical World View*
World, Nature	The changeless physical universe is ordered according to mechanistic "laws of nature" which yield predictable effects from given causes. Time is a linear phenomenon, moving at a fixed, constant pace. Material objects fill the space they occupy.	Physical universe is in constant change. Nothing is permanent, nothing concrete. Rather than natural laws, there are natural paradoxes and "unions of opposites." Time is not linear. Cause-effect relationships are mental creations, not a function of the material world.

Table A: Summary Overview of Eastern and Western World Views (Continued)

	Western, Materialistic World View	*Eastern, Mystical World View*
Knowledge	Knowledge is focused on unchanging "essences" of material objects. True knowledge (*episteme*) is a true copy of the material object or phenomenon in the mind of the observer.	Ultimate reality can never be an object of reasoning or "demonstrable" knowledge. It can never be described adequately in words or pictures. The mind knows more than what is at the focus of consciousness
Method	The method of science seeks for truth in cause-effect relationships between physical forces and material objects. Proof, evidence, truth, is external to the observer, residing in the material objects and their cause-effect relationships.	Absolute knowledge is an entirely non-intellectual experience of reality that arises out of a non-ordinary state of consciousness, a meditative or mystical state.

A Western, Non-Rational View of the World

Almost simultaneously with the discoveries in atomic research that introduced serious doubts about the validity of the Western, positive science, world view, there appeared some dissident voices in European literature which strongly critiqued the materialistic focus of Western culture. The criticisms were not based upon religious nor mystical grounds. The argument was straightforward and simple: from the point of view of the common man, the world seems to be neither orderly nor predictable. Most events affecting personal lives seem not to obey simple cause-effect rules. Rather, they are beyond us, eluding any comprehensive understanding or individual control.

Over a half-century, a number of European writers undertook to present the *human* view of the lived-world, as contrasted with the *materialistic* view that was the focus of the scientific paradigm. Eventually, this collection of literature, music, and theater arts came to be labeled "existentialism," perhaps from a phrase in Jean Paul Sartre's writings which became popularized: *"Existence precedes essence."* The phrase was generally interpreted to mean that our *existence* as human beings should be considered to be of higher priority than knowing the *essence* of material objects, a passion that for centuries had been the thrust of Western science and philosophy.

As it developed, existential philosophy departed decisively from the positive science view of a mechanistic, cause-effect ordered world. In effect, it threatened the dominant positive science paradigm, strongly criticizing the materialistic focus of Western culture. Existentialism presents a usefully alternative view of what the world is like, and how it should be conceptualized from the point of view of *human existence.* In the section that follows, we describe this alternative view in the form of existential categories for describing and understanding the "world" we live in. We continue with an application of these ideas to the day-to-day world of the manager.

Chapter 5:
An Existential Paradigm

Classical philosophy comes to an end in Hegel, because it has become folly to construct intellectual totalitarian systems in which everything is taken up, harmonized, rationalized, and justified. Such palaces are still marvelous, but nobody can live in them. The savor and reality of human existence, its perils and triumphs, its bitterness and sweetness, are outside in the street.

—Simone de Beauvoir, Pour une morale de l'ambiguité.

What you will find in this chapter

1. **The philosophical roots of existentialism**

2. **Existential categories for understanding the world**

3. **Authenticity, self-actualization, and decision making**

The evolution of existentialism

In a marked divergence from the positive science paradigm then dominant in all of Europe, existential writing began as a rebellion against the philosophical status quo in Europe, and proposed a radically different vision of man in the universe. There was no coherent philosophical framework developed to channel the rebellion. Their writings seemed to emerge spontaneously from personally felt frustrations at the recognition that human existence was being overlooked in a paradigm of material science.

To give the reader a sense of this alternative worldview, we synthesize core concepts selected from the writings of several authors, and present them in the form of conceptual categories that describe the existential way of viewing the world. The categories discussed come mainly from the writings of Sören Kierkegaard, Martin Heidegger, and Jean-Paul Sartre.

We believe that each of these categories has implications for the manager concerned with the people in his organization. They can offer an alternative way of understanding how they themselves may perceive the world they live in, together with some insights about how people feel about the values and fears that motivate them and the people with whom they work. In the concept of *authenticity* we find a basis for a moral tone in management and in manager-worker relationships.

Existential Categories for Understanding the World

1. Absurdity—the Condition of the World

People, and especially managers, have a deep psychological need to see *order* in the events which shape their lives. When life appears to be ordered, predictable, one can understand the meaning of events, and respond with confidence. In Western civilization, these ideas of orderliness have been based upon a system of science-based knowledge that postulates an ordered universe possessing built-in "laws of nature," including presumed cause-effect relationships which help to explain events in the physical world.

The existential description of the lived-world departs sharply from this familiar positive-science paradigm, emphasizing that at least the human aspects of one's existence are not orderable by scientific or rational rules. Dostoevsky and Kafka, named among the earliest existential writers, used literature to describe the plight of the common man caught up in a series of events in which the events themselves, whether bizarre or commonplace, were beyond the control of the person in the story, or circumstances were such that it seemed impossible to respect existing rules of the game if one wanted to live authentically.

Other early writers, including Kierkegaard, and especially, Nietzche, advocated tearing down the existing order and its symbols so that a more human and "natural" order of things might emerge. A half century later, Sartre and Camus continued this nihilistic theme by labeling the existing world as "absurd," that is, without any intrinsic meaning. By characterizing the world as absurd, these writers carry on a theme common to existentialists: a profound disenchantment with science, accompanied by attempts to free mankind from superstitious over-confidence in science, or religion, or in philosophical systems which pretend to furnish knowledge.

We might summarize this view of the world in a line from Dostoevsky's *Notes from the Underground*:

> *In short, one may say anything about the history of the world—anything that might enter the most disordered imagination. The only thing one can't say is that it's rational.*[1]

2. Facticity—the Factual Elements of One's Existence

Heidegger points out that man awakens to his existence, having been "cast" or "thrown " into a world that he did not create, and at a time that he did not choose. This most factual element of our existence is a given; one we cannot modify. Part of our *facticity* is the physical environment we live in; part of it is our socio-economic heritage. The only materials we are given to work with as we fashion our own existence are based in this physical world *facticity*.

3. Existentiality—Everyman's Enterprise

By *existentiality*, Heidegger means to say that although we awaken to a world we did not create and at a time not of our choosing, the "stuff" of the material world is there for our use. From it, we must, each of us, fashion a life that is worth living. Heidegger calls this our "existential project"—that is, one's life project is to begin with the personal facticity of the physical world wherein we have been cast, and out of it fashion a life worth living. Our existentiality, then, is expressed in the ways in which we take the givens of our world and fashion them into a meaningful existence.

4. Authenticity—Man's Highest Objective

The principal objective in working out one's existential project is to be authentic. Living an authentic existence includes creating a happy combination of external elements which constitute one's facticity, together with those very personal

---

1. Dostoevsky, quoted in Walter A. Kaufmann, (ed.) *Existentialism from Dostoevsky to Sartre.* (NY: Meridian Books, World Pub. Co., 1956) p.75

desires and expressions of the self which lie at the core of one's being, such that one's existence becomes a legitimate expression of what one has proposed to be. Above all, in the existential ranking of values, one must *be authentic* in bringing one's life-project into focus around a set of roles that represent the self as we really are. The student of managerial psychology will find parallels between the concept of authenticity and Abraham Maslow's idea of "self-actualization."

5. Freedom and Choice—Everyman's Horizon of Opportunity

The existential description of man's conditions of freedom is radically different from that developed by Rousseau and Freud, who argued that every man is severely limited in his self-expression by the restraints of society and its institutions. The line, *"Man is born free, but everywhere he is in chains,"* was Rousseau's opening statement of an argument to the effect that man is basically noble in instinct and intent, but unfortunately, societal institutions corrupt that nobility. He argued that churches, schools, government, society, community, and the family—all teach, and attempt to enforce, a set of obligations and restrictions that have the cumulative effect of severely restricting individual freedom of choice and action. Freud developed this idea much more deeply in his *Civilization and Its Discontents*.[2]

The existential authors turn this argument upside down. Both Kierkegaard and Sartre declare that man is actually so unfettered that the awareness of the scope of his freedoms causes him great anxiety, since to be completely free means to be personally responsible for each of his own choices, actions, and ultimately, his own destiny.[3] In the events of every day, the individual is forced to make choices with too little knowledge of the outcomes, which, it can be understood, is a source of considerable anxiety. Sartre describes how each of us invents excuses and plays out mental scenarios so that we will not have to choose between difficult or ambiguous alternatives. We make excuses for not changing habits of action that do not give optimal results, and we play mind games so that we can comfortably follow the crowd, letting others make the choices for us and thereby carry the responsibility for the outcomes.

---

2.   Sigmund Freud, *Civilization and Its Discontents*. NY: Dover Publications, Inc. 1930, 1994

3.   Rollo May, *Escape From Freedom*.

A relatively large portion of the existential literature is devoted to discussions of man's freedom and how he handles it. The two categories that follow, *Forfeiture* and *Bad Faith*, were developed by Sartre, and help to illustrate some of the thinking characterizing this literature.

6. Forfeiture—Let the Others Decide…

Usually it is easier to follow the crowd, to let others make the choices rather than to struggle with the ambivalences of a truly authentic choice. When I follow the crowd rather than using my own faculties to optimize my authenticity, I am in a state of forfeiture, according to Sartre.

Kierkegaard, in more dramatic language, declared that "truth" is never found with the majority; to follow the crowd means to live a lie.

> *The multitude is a lie; not this or that multitude, of rich or poor, living or dead, of high or low, but the multitude itself, viewed as a category, for it always gives unaccountability and irresponsibility.*[4]

In the existential lexicon, then, forfeiture means letting others make decisions for us. It means an uncritical following of the majority, the crowd; doing what "they" do without questioning whether it is the right thing, or the authentic thing, to do.

7. Bad Faith—When I Lie to Myself

Sartre also develops the concept of *mauvaise foie*, or bad faith, defining it as the all-too-human habit of inventing excuses or "mind-games" to keep from having to bear the personal responsibility of living with one's choices. The games exist in endless variety, but all are, at base, excuses I make to myself in which I say things like, "That is impossible (for me);" "They would never allow me to do that;" "Such and such could never work out," etc. Each time I use such an excuse to keep from making a conscious choice to act authentically, I am acting instead "in bad faith."

---

4.   Sören Kierkegaard, *The Point of View for My Work As An Author,* in David F. Swenson, *Something About Kierkegaard,* (Minneapolis, MN: Augsburg Publishing House, 1941) p.31

Note, please, that bad faith is inward, towards me; it is not the same as hypocrisy, or cheating, which is a kind of bad faith toward other persons. The outcome of bad faith is that I excuse myself from the responsibility of bearing the risks associated with acting authentically by placing the blame on external factors. It is the authenticity of my own existential project which I am thereby compromising.

8. Anxiety—Everyman's Intimate Companion

Nearly all existential authors discuss the ubiquity of anxiety in the human experience, although under different names and with differing explanations as to its genesis and consequences. Kierkegaard calls it "dread" or "finitude"—an awareness that we are finite and expendable, and that someday, probably not one of our choosing, our existence will be ended without us having accomplished much of note.

Sartre labels it *nausée* (nausea), while the German authors call it *angst*. Experientially, it can best be described as the knot of fear or anxiousness felt in the pit of the stomach when one faces the unpredictable or the unknown. Sartre seems to argue that this gut-level anxiety is the common denominator of all human self-awareness, the trade-mark, so to speak, of being human.

The framework of science has long argued that man's rationality defines the gulf between human and other life forms. Existential authors agree that man can be rational, but also argue that the universal fact of human existence is the anxiety of having to make choices with insufficient knowledge of their outcomes.

9. Truth

We can come to grips with the existential idea of truth most quickly by citing a brief statement found in the journals of Sören Kierkegaard:

> *What I really need is clearness as to what I ought to do; not so much as to what I ought to know, except insofar as some form of knowledge precedes all doing. I need a truth that is a truth for me; an idea for which I can live and die. What I need is the power to live a complete human life, not merely a life of knowledge, in order that my thought might not merely be based on something objective, something not my own, but rather on something connected with the deepest root of my existence. Something through which I am linked to the divine, and to which I could cling if the whole world were to fall in ruins about me.*[5]

For Kierkegaard, truth does not exist as an objective reality external to the person; truth is to be found deep in the soul of the individual. The reader will recall from earlier passages that Kierkegaard makes a sharp cleavage between the individual and the multitude or crowd. Forfeiture, you will recall, comes from following the crowd and its norms rather than doing what is necessary in order to be authentic. Truth, then, is related to personal authenticity; one doesn't *say* the truth; one *does* the truth. Truth is a fundamental category of one's authentic existence as expressed in one's actions. It is *an idea for which I can live and die,* transcending mere knowledge, and transcending any given context.

The careful reader will note the similarity between the existential insistence upon *"a truth for me"* and the teachings of Eastern philosophy which hold that *absolute knowledge* is an entirely non-intellectual experience of reality which arises out of a non-ordinary state of consciousness, is entirely personal, and cannot be represented in words.

Although there are important cultural differences in the way the human search for enlightenment is pursued in East and West, nevertheless, a number of the ideas found in existentialism may be thought of as the West's creation of its own version of a world view long held by Eastern cultures. It offers a useful alternative to the contemporary Western "scientific" view of the world.

Most important for managers, existentialism's emphasis on living *authentically* can give rise to a set of ethical guidelines for making choices and decisions when it is difficult to possess full knowledge of the situation and its alternatives, human factors are involved, and there is uncertainty about outcomes.

---

5.   Cited in David F. Swenson, *Something About Kierkegaard.* Minneapolis: Augsburg Publishing House, 1941. p.40

Chapter 6:
The Existential Manager

The GODS had condemned Sisyphus to ceaselessly rolling a rock to the top of a mountain, whence the stone would fall back of its own weight. They had thought with some reason that there is no more dreadful punishment than futile and hopeless labor.

If one believes Homer, Sisyphus was the wisest and most prudent of mortals.

—Albert Camus, *The Myth of Sisyphus.*

What you will find in this chapter

1. **The existential versus rationalistic frameworks**

2. **Existential categories and their implications for the managerial roles**

3. **Paradigm competence versus absence of paradigms**

Existential versus rationalistic frameworks

The existential framework offers the promise of a more true-to-life description of the human aspects of organizational life than does the rationalistic framework of positive science. It can highlight human wants and needs, focus on valued objectives, and help in the development of a sense of a meaningful existence for individuals. An existential framework is helpful to formulate guidelines for the manager in making choices and decisions, for himself, as well as for others. The categories discussed above relate to a manager's life and work in some of the following illustrative ways.

Managerial Facticity

Take the concept of *"facticity,"* for example. Many managers have had the experience of having to create a functioning organization out of whatever is at hand. He cannot always insist upon having a larger budget or new resources to cope with new problems, but must make do with the physical and human resources he inherits. The resourceful manager looks for creative ways to make the system function with what is available to him and his group. Occasionally he learns the important insight that his main contribution as a leader is to develop and communicate the idea of what can be achieved by collective effort, in spite of the obvious resource lacks.

There is no question that the traditional scientific framework yields good results when applied to purely physical world problems, ones that can be treated by the engineering sciences, for example. To the extent that the problem under analysis can be restricted to purely physical objects or materials, there is no need to look for another conceptual framework.

But in managerial decisions in which human factors are important, it seems valid to employ a completely different framework that is oriented toward human needs and human meanings. The existential world view seems better to capture the nuances of human needs and motivations, and can yield important insights into the motivations of employees.

Existential Project

The concept of *"existential project"*—of everyone's need to fashion a "life worth living" out of the raw materials of one's existence, seems appropriate to some managerial problems. At the organization level, for instance, the manager's project is to create and/or modify in the minds of his coworkers the concept of the organizational project or goal. He may express it in a variety of ways; experiential, verbal, or graphic, but it must seem worthy of being lived by each of the employees or their individual motivation will be low and their cooperation mediocre.

The Authentic Manager

At the managerial level there is a certain charisma about a leader who is able to present himself as *an authentic person.* That authenticity lends legitimacy to his formal authority role, and is like money in the bank when it comes to asking for the cooperation of those who work for him.

However, the corollary of being an authentic manager is that he must be willing to treat his employees as authentic individuals in their own right, which means giving them a voice in decisions that affect their work and welfare. Self-expression that is encouraged can yield extraordinary benefits in creative responses by the group in helping to solve unpredictable problems that are the bane of every manager.

We are suggesting that giving consideration to the employee's need to be authentic as an individual is a cornerstone of employee motivation; that it constitutes a necessary prerequisite for application, in the work place, of the methods developed in organizational psychology for the motivation of workers.

Choice in a Context of Unbounded Freedom

Charles Reich writes that the current generation in America knows something that previous generations did not know—that it is really possible to choose surfing on a California beach over a job in a factory without necessarily starving to death as a consequence.[1] This kind of insight produces a need for a different kind of motivation rationale on the part of managers in today's work place, for neither the offer of increased pay nor the threat of termination yields the expected results for the employee whose goal is to be authentic.

In contrast to older, traditional values, Anders Richter writes that the factors which characterize *existential choices* are *optimism* even in times of dark uncertainty, *open-mindedness,* in the sense of being prepared to alter choices on the basis of fresh information, and *empathy,* which recognizes that we impute choices to others on the basis of our own subjective feelings.[2] Behind all this stands the idea that with every choice, the manager is dramatizing his own personality with the actions he takes.

Bureaucratic Bad Faith

Bad faith means using excuses drawn from outside one's self to keep from facing the need for a decision or choice, while *forfeiture* means uncritically following the crowd, or tradition, or old habits, to avoid taking personal responsibility for a

1.   Charles A. Reich, *The Greening of America,* (NY: Random House, 1970)
2.   Anders Richter, "The Existentialist Executive," (**PAR**, Jul/Aug, 1970) p.417

decision. Both of these existential "sins" have their bureaucratic manifestations in the syndrome known as "hiding behind the regulations" to keep from taking personal responsibility for actions or decisions. This is particularly true in the management of human resources, where supervisors and managers tend to use regulations to explain or to justify personnel actions for which they do not wish to take personal responsibility.

The Anxious Bureaucrat

The most common forms of allaying this ubiquitous human anxiety are expressed in everyday bureaucratic behaviors in the organization. There is the search for security of employment in seniority, in formal position; there is the hiding behind the regulations rather than risking a personal decision, or the routines of getting one's superior to sign off on memos of action to be taken; there is the impersonal face of the role-playing administrator which is presented to clients and subordinates, a mask so that the anxiety will not be revealed to the rest of the world.

One of the painful outcomes of human attempts to hide personal anxieties behind the façade of a formalized managerial role in an organization. This was characterized by Victor Thompson as a "bureaupathology" leading to an institutional illness he called "bureausis." When managers act out their personal fears by inauthentically clothing themselves in their assigned organizational role because they do not dare to act in a personally authentic way, Thompson points out that they are introducing pathological consequences into the organizational bureaucracy. If such inauthentic behavior is widespread, the entire organization is suffering from a "bureausis."

Concluding:

Permit us to end **Part I** with a portion of a short text written by a friend who is a professor and consultant who designs and presents programs for executive development. At first he called them, *"Horizons and Frontiers,"* but later renamed his executive development programs *"Horizons Without Frontiers."* The writer's purpose in this text portion is not paradigm competence; rather how to function without paradigm limitations. But let him speak for himself:

> *"I am what I think, what I think (judge) to be true. What I think is limited by my rational and non-rational beliefs with respect to the world. My creative thoughts*

flow from what I think. Please note that here I do not consider thinking in the Cartesian conception of "Cogito, ergo sum" [I think, therefore I exist], because this "Cogito" speaks with respect to rational, discursive thinking of the left hemisphere. When I say "think," I understand a global expression, something like a complex hologram, interpreting another hologram: an illusory reality that we "think" to be an absolute reality.

My paradigms, constituted of limiting beliefs, determine my creativity. When I understand the limits, when I have the courage to deal with the unknown, thereby generating wider paradigms, I augment my potential for creative action. Revolution (the creation of a new paradigm) implies "more energy" than evolution (the creation within a paradigm). In general, we associate more energy with something that involves a longer time (or difficulty). This has meaning when we move in serial (CHRONOS) time, yet the creative process does not necessarily involve "perspiration," because it is situated in "leap" time—KAIROS that comes from the Greek APEIRON (absolute). In summary, the creative process occurs in an "elastic" time that can be stretched out at our pleasure, that is, in the measure that we believe necessary.

We can say our "quantity" or "quality" of creation is a function of the amplitude of the paradigm that we use in our "weltanschaang" (world view). If our horizons do not have frontiers—i.e., limits—neither will our creativity have frontiers. Since all paradigms have limits because they are logically structured, a creation without limits only occurs in the absence of paradigms. Because of this, we must break out of our logical prisons, as do the masters of Zen in their "Koans." As the Bodhidharma, the founding patriarch of Zen is supposed to have said: "I am an absurd man…I would wish to cut off your head…because I want to hear you speak from your heart."[3]

---

3.   We refer to Carlos Pradel Azevedo, a biologist with several published books in his area of specialization. He also has a post-graduate degree in education.

PART II
Managing Oneself

o o o o o o o o o o o o o o o o o o o o o o o o o o o o o o o o o o

*People say I am crazy to do what I am doing. And they offer all kinds
of advice to save me from ruin. When I tell them that I am O.K.,
they look at me strangely. "Certainly you are not happy now that you
are not participating in the game…" People formulate questions that
are lost in the confusion. I tell them there are no problems, only solutions.*

—John Lennon
Watching the Wheels. 1980

Introduction

"Know Thyself"[1]

We believe sincerely that the best organizations—the most efficient, effectual and effective—are capable of surviving in the midst of today's turbulence. We further believe that what organizations propose to achieve depends upon people who are the most integrated[2], the most capable of managing their own lives. They will also be among the most satisfied and actualized. This combination is what we have proposed as the desired objective of *ReAdministration*, that is, organizations of high performance staffed by individuals who are satisfied and actualized.

The following concerns are linked with how to go about initiating such a process. When we spoke of improving organizations, we said that the starting point should be a diagnosis: "If the organization does not know where it is, nor where it intends to arrive, it doesn't have any chance of successfully surviving the contemporary turbulence."[3]

This is not much different with relation to the individuals: self-reflection, and the process of self-knowledge, has to mark the beginning of this journey.

In this act of "going into oneself" (interiorization) we have come across the work of numerous authors and scholars that has been helpful. From among these, we have chosen a model called *"mental cartography"* developed by Roberto Assagioli, the father of *psychosynthesis,* which we have selected because of its simplicity. Since a model does not necessarily have to be true, but only useful—after all, this is the pragmatic view of an administrator. The selection of Assagioli's model proves to be valuable in the structuring of **Part II** of this book: which deals with the notions of *consciousness, unconsciousness,* and *interface* between them. Even though these concepts did not originate with him, he has developed them usefully.

---

1. *"Nosce te ipsum"* (Sócrates) "Know thyself"
2. INTEGRAL, whole, essential completeness
3. Geraldo Caravantes and Wesley Bjur, *ReAdministração em Ação.* São Paulo: Makron Books, 1996, p.97

Under each of these three headings we have attempted to develop a few topics related to our criteria in order to exemplify and illustrate concepts capable of organizing and synthesizing ideas judged to be relevant, concepts capable of contributing to the growth of the reader; and in a form capable of maintaining a degree of interest which will stimulate further reading.

Assagioli: A Model to Explore our Interior World

Today many, perhaps a majority, of persons feel unsatisfied with the kind of life they are living and they search, with a certain eagerness, for something different, something out of the ordinary, or common-place. The search for a resolution of this lack of satisfaction generally follows either of two routes: the first conducts the person in search of new knowledge about the external world and in the conquest of new areas or spaces. We have already gone to the moon. Why not to Mars or Jupiter next?

The second is usually connected to the expansion of knowledge related to our interior world. Perhaps better said, our interior worlds. The growing interest in psychology for the study of the unconscious exemplifies this second route. Both can contribute to the expansion of consciousness.

Assagioli proposes the following diagram that can have surprising didactic value.

According to Assagioli's portrayal, the expansion of consciousness can be developed in three directions:

1) downward, 2) horizontally, and 3) upward.

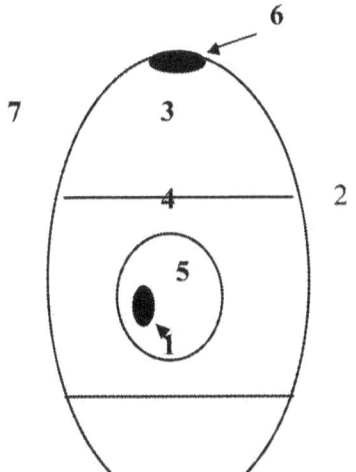

1. The Inferior Unconscious
2. Intermediate Unconscious
3. Superior Unconscious, or "Superconscious"
4. Area of Consciousness
5. I-Consciousness; the Self
6. The Superior Self
7. The Collective Unconscious

Roberto Assagioli, *Transpersonal Development,* San Francisco: The Aquarian Press, 1993. p. 24

Downward: Giving emphasis to the development of the inferior (lower) unconscious. This is the field of deep psychology and especially of psychoanalysis. The development of this area is normally carried on for educational or therapeutic reasons. However, some feel a special attraction for certain aspects that are questionable, such as a fascination for the most primitive and instinctive aspects of human beings, including the horrific.

Horizontally: When the expansion of consciousness contemplates the participation and identification with others as with nature and with things that surround us. Its result is a feeling of total integration with the universe.

Upward: In the direction of the level of the Superconscious. The expansion of consciousness can be experienced in two manners. The first consists in raising the center of consciousness, the I-Consciousness, toward higher levels; the second is to open oneself to the influence of energies emanating from those levels.

To expand how the I-Consciousness (Number 5 in the diagram) works in an effective manner in the area of the Conscious (Number 4 in the diagram), we choose four topics to be treated in following sections: a) the concept of *rationality*, b) the *paradoxes* of management, c) the notion of *personal planning*, and d) a discussion about *learning to learn*.

Our premise is that: a) if one can operate with an amplified rationality (not merely functional rationality, with a focus on *means* and a predetermined objective); b) if one is capable of using this amplified rationality to better plan one's personal life; c) and finally, if one can incorporate the notion of learning as a continual process necessary to survival (your own, that of the organization in which you work, and of society as a whole) then, undoubtedly, you will be managing your own consciousness in an adequate manner.

But on the other hand, why be content with so little? Your existence is more than your conscious element. Look again at the diagram of Assagioli. Perhaps you are able to take hold and make use of resources which have accumulated in your unconscious and that might be of great value to improve your life. We refer not merely to your bookish and intellectualized life, but to your entire personal life, the sum of your inquiries, practices, investigations, and lived-experiences.

There are technologies available to help one utilize this fountain of material from our unconscious, and more, they have important applications in stress management. The technology we have chosen for our purposes in Chapter 8 is Hypnosis, which has more than a century of applied use. We will write about it, giving examples as students and practitioners, in the hope of bringing to administrators some ideas to which they, with high probability, have not been previously exposed. In other words, something old, but at the same time, something new and useful.

In Chapter 9, *Rational Intuition or Intuitive Reason,* we attempt to show how inspiration, intuition and creativity give rise to the interplay between the conscious and the unconscious. Our challenge, when we understand the nature of this interrelationship, is to elevate personal growth based upon both conscious and unconscious elements.

Assagioli employs a useful metaphor when he points out that an acorn contains all the potential to become a mighty oak tree, with all of its grandness, but the acorn should never think of itself as already being a mighty oak. Similarly, humans, using only their conscious mind, cannot hope to become the *opus magnum* of creation, "in the image and likeness of God."

In Chapter 10 we deal further with what Assagioli has called the *superior unconscious* or the *superconscious,* that which Maslow called *transpersonality.* (Assagioli used also the word *spirituality* as an equivalent to *transpersonality.*) What the authors want to propose is that we ought not to permit ourselves to be less than what effectively we can be: a mere acorn, for instance, when we have the potential to "germinate" and develop, becoming (metaphorically) a monumental oak.

We return, in summary, to a metaphor which we have used in an earlier work: man, considered earlier as a mere "surfer" riding the waves, might better be considered as a part of the ocean itself, indistinguishable from it, an ocean which extends itself as far as it can cover the sands of its shores.

To summarize, remember that the terms *conscious, unconscious,* and *superconscious* are mere adjective forms referring to portions of the human mind. This is to remind us that they are "temporary expressions of a psychological nature, and not stand-alone entities."[4]

---

4.   Roberto Assagioli, *Transpersonal Development,* San Francisco: The Aquarian Press, 1993. p. 24

Chapter 7:
Managing the Conscious

Son:	*Father, why don't you use the other three-quarters of your mind?*
Father:	*Well, the problem is that I had professors who filled about a quarter of my brain with cobwebs. After that I read journals and listened to what other people said. This filled another quarter with a dense fog.*
Son:	*And the other quarter, father?*
Father:	*O, this is the confusion that I myself have generated when I have attempted to think.*

—Gregory Bateson, *Metadiálogos.*

What you will find in this chapter

1. **What does it mean to be rational?**

2. **Paradoxes of managing: planning the unplannable**

3. **Individual planning**

4. **Learning to learn**

1. WHAT DOES IT MEAN TO BE RATIONAL?[1]

We can agree that an individual, a social system, or an organization, all are able to recognize that they can usually acquire the capacity for new behaviors. However, our society seems to exhibit a complete incapacity to generate creative solutions to the principal problems that we confront in this beginning of a new century. We continue to face emerging problems with inadequate, obsolete, or insufficient solutions. As a consequence, serious problems continue to accumulate and feelings of abandonment and perplexity have become principal characteristics of our contemporary world.

Substantive versus Functional Rationality

We believe that one of the ways in which we might help to clarify this perplexity, in search of valid alternatives, is by pointing out the differences between *substantive and functional rationality*, because of their implications for the larger society in which we live.

Substantive Rationality.

Reason, in its classical meaning, is one of the premier functions of the human mind. It is reason which permits individuals to make ethical and sound judgments about personal and social life. Eric Voegelin affirms that reason is a human dimension that cannot be considered as belonging to history or to a society. Reason transcends history and society, belonging exclusively to the individual human psyche. Reason, therefore, in its classical or substantive meaning, has nothing to do with the characteristics of an epoch or any specific society. In reality, substantive rationality assumes a dichotomy between *reason* and *society*. An intrinsic component of human nature, it is reason which permits people to be liberated from specific social and historical episodes of their history, and to seek the general good by means of a constant warring against human passions.[2]

---

1.   In collaboration with Professor María José Lara de Bretas Pereira
2.   Eric Voegelin, quoted in A. Guerreiro Ramos, *The New Science of Organizations*. Toronto: University of Toronto Press, 1982

Max Weber, in his *Economy and Society*,[3] marks the ways in which social policies can be oriented. He suggests four basic ways: 1) using substantive rationality (which includes values), 2) using instrumental rationality (focused on means), 3) based on affective issues, and 4) holding on to the traditional. Weber's focus was concentrated principally on functional rationality.

Karl Mannheim, in his work, *Man and Society in an Age of Reconstruction*,[4] is one who best explores the substantive or valorative aspect of reason/rationality. For him, substantive rationality (i.e., reason in its full sense) is an act of thinking that reveals an intelligent *insight* about the interrelationships of events in a given situation.

We can conclude from his work that substantive rationality, or human reason, is directly linked to the critical capacity man possesses to reflect on himself and his actions. It is exactly this capacity of self-reflection, of self-observation and evaluation of the situation which permits one to constantly recapitulate and prepare to face unexpected and unforeseen events. This critical posture makes man not a mere product of, but rather a critical participant in, a given historical period. Substantive rationality implies the fact that individuals—the bearers of reason—will be the subjects of the process of learning.

Functional Rationality.

The modern concept of reason/rationality was probably best systematized by Hobbes in his *Leviathan*. For Hobbes, rationality is not merely a capacity of human nature, but is a quality man acquires by means of his own efforts and which capacitates him to evaluate the consequences of choices made.[5]

If we return once more to the Greeks, we encounter in Aristotle an even better explanation of what we here call functional rationality:

> *You do not ask a medical doctor if he will or will not cure his patient, an orator if he will or will not convince his audience, or a statesman if he should strive for good government. They take their final objective as a certainty and decide how and by which means they will be able to achieve that objective. If they discover that there*

3. Max Weber, *Economy and Society: An Outline of Interpretative Sociology.* University of California Press, 1978, Vol. 1
4. Karl Mannheim, *Man and Society in an Age of Reconstruction.* New York: Harcourt, Brace & World, 1940
5. Thomas Hobbes, *Leviathan.* New York: The Free Press, 1976

are different manners by which to achieve it, they go on to consider which of these means can achieve the objective in the best or easiest way.[6]

The latter part of Aristotle's affirmation agrees perfectly with what Herbert Simon affirms in his book, *Administrative Behavior:*

Fact and value...these are the relationships between means and ends. In the decision process we select alternatives considered as the means best indicated to achieve the objectives desired. The objectives themselves, however, are no more than instruments used to obtain better defined objectives. We thus arrive at the concept of an hierarchical series of objectives. Rationality is related to the construction of chains of means and ends of this type.[7]

The "derailment" of reason

In the rise of the "modern era"—now around 200 years old—the classical sense of *reason* was lost to Western culture in a process that Voegelin labels *derailment.*[8] For the Greeks, the distinction between substantive and functional rationality was clear. *Reason* was used to clarify and decide long-term, substantive, valued issues touching such things as home and family, while *rationality* was limited to decisions made in the marketplace; for instance, in deciding how to get the biggest and best bunch of carrots for the lowest price.

With the passage of time, Voegelin and others argue, this distinction was lost to Western society. For a majority of authors and modern theorists, *rationality* came to be the substitute for *reason,* and today *functional rationality* remains the only concept existing to define the field of human reason/rationality. How this could occur is explained in part by the industrial revolution, where there prevailed an utilitarian philosophy that opened the way to utilitarian practices, carrying with them a distorted vision of man and society as a whole.

The economic fallacy of a market mentality

The *economic fallacy* defined by Karl Polanyi[9] is an example of this idea. During the past century, neoclassical economics and its definition of rationality became

---

6.   Aristotle, *Nichomachean Ethics*. London: William Heineman, 1975
7.   Herbert Simon, *Administrative Behavior*. New York: The Free Press, 1976
8.   Eric Voegelin, *"Reason: The Classical Experience,"* in The Southern Review, Spring, 1974
9.   Karl Polanyi, *The Livelihood of Man*. New York: Academic Press, 1977

the only acceptable form by which to analyze the history of humankind. The mentality of the market, which had had little significant influence of in the world prior to the XIX Century, became the parameter by which all history comes to be analyzed: In the market society, resources, needs, and equivalencies are substituted for offer, demand, and prices, respectively. In other words, a social reality that used to include substantive values, guided by reason, has given way to a kind of "rational" market-related fiction.

This point of false reference came to be considered as the "real world," an imaginary world with Adam Smith as its architect. From Thomas Hobbes to Adam Smith's *Theory of Moral Sentiments,* the classical meaning of *reason*, which earlier had been the principal parameter for the orientation of human existence, was substituted by a new definition of *rationality*. This market-related definition of reason/rationality no longer presupposes any control of passions by the human will, but rather the will is put at the service of those very passions. The *good* came to be substituted by the *functional,* functional being always defined in utilitarian terms. In other words, "the inherent exigencies of the market have been converted into rationality, thus defined."[10]

This functional rationality, based in an utilitarian evaluation of the consequences of human action, lacks any ethical qualification whatever, because it applies to conduct only in whatever sense conduct is recognized as a means, a means to achieve a determined objective. Means and ends come to be the only referral point with respect to human behavior. Learning, in this context, comes to be synonymous with the capacity to acquire the techniques and abilities necessary to achieve a specified end, whatever that end might be. While there is nothing inherently wrong with this logic, yet it must be classified as an incomplete framework, because considerations of an ethical order are not taken into account in the quest for desired objectives.

Substantive and functional rationality contrasted.

The difference between these two types of rationality appears frequently in modern administration. Both are always present in our ways of perceiving and elaborating our own vision of the world. The problem arises when there is an unbalanced utilization of the two, whether in personal or social terms. Many of the negative traits that people evidence in a bureaucratic setting are the result of their fondness for functional rationality, arriving, at times, to extremes in which

---

10.   A. Guerreiro Ramos, *The New Science of Organizations,* op. cit.

agency clients are reduced to simple number identifiers, and where the emotional tone, to use the words of Victor Thompson,[11] "is the complete lack of compassion."

However, in a pragmatic sense substantive rationality is not always preferable over functional rationality. An example given by Robert Miedwald serves to clarify this point:

> *If by chance we were to find our postman seated on the curb, meditating over a paper on the cosmic scheme of things, we would probably shout that he should get busy and deliver the mail. One ought also to doubt that a political organization could long survive only on the basis of substantive rationality.*[12]

We conclude, therefore, that we may consider ourselves fortunate that administrators are not philosophers because if they were, there could be a lot of time lost in meditating upon insoluble metaphysical problems, never completing a given task.

The differences between functional and substantive rationality can be summarized and compared in the following table, using variables considered the most relevant by a majority of authors.

Variable	Functional Rationality	Substantive Rationality
Application (how things are done in practice)	Getting things done depends upon the contingencies of the process	Choice of means is intrinsic to the individual, having a normative, rather than a contingent quality.
The sequence of means and ends	Presupposes a preestablished objective, and concentrates on the application of efficient means to achieve that end.	Presupposes the existence of efficient means, but concentrates on the choice and selection of objectives and goals.
Relations between process and content	Gives emphasis to process and ignores the content.	Gives emphasis to the content, but not to the process.

---

11. Victor Thompson, *Without Sympathy or Enthusiasm—The Problem of Administrative Compassion.* Alabama: The University of Alabama Press, 1975
12. Robert Miedwald, *Public Administration, a Critical Perspective.* New York: McGraw-Hill, 1978

Variable	Functional Rationality	Substantive Rationality
Human existence in society	Subordinates human objectives to the operational requisites of the society	Subordinates operational requisites of the society to human needs and objectives.

Society's loss of a rational balance

Analyzing the work of important social critics such as Marcuse, Horkheimer, and especially those affiliated with the Frankfurt School, we find at least one common element among their criticisms—they denounce the loss, society-wide, of a balance between substantive and functional rationality. This loss dates from the beginning of the Industrial Revolution, when the predominance of functional rationality began to impose itself into all areas of social life.

It is not difficult to identify the basic reasons underlying the success achieved by a society based on functionalism: it has been capable of providing us with an abundance of consumer goods required, on an increasing scale, by the market society. Take, for example, the United States, without doubt the first nation in the history of humanity which, by means of the massive application of technology (soft and hard) has been able to feed, clothe, and offer the comforts of modern life to more than 260 million people, employing for such purposes only 3% of the active working force in agriculture and about 25% in industry. With all of this running like clockwork, why should we pose the question, "What is there to worry about?"

The fact that there continue to exist problems which, although they have been identified for many years, are only now being faced as critical issues. The continually expanding industrialization presupposes an emphasis upon functional rationality, the better to organize the activities of a society with these consumer-oriented objectives.

At the same time, however, the society has not given a similar emphasis to substantive rationality, a condition inviting criticism given the need for the kind of learning that permits the society to transcend the standards of market-related behavior now so well established. In reality, the collective capacity for reasoning, in the classical sense, has been seriously inhibited, as we will see farther along. Large organizations (with their administrators) have created a narrow view of rationality which Herbert Simon labeled "limited rationality."[13]

---

13.   Simon, *op. cit.*

This is a functional vision of the world that does not include all possible variables, but rather offers only a number of premises that members of the organization can cope with. What effectively happens is that organizations offer their members a structure which dictates for them what exists and what does not exist. This type of rationality, although imperfect and incomplete, admittedly functions very well in practice. The consequence of this functionalism—and this is the number one problem—is that in a functionalist society, a complete understanding of the complex sequence of actions is limited to a few administrative leaders, which assures to these persons key positions in the society. They are specialists, technocrats, or "professors;" those who know and have the responsibility to teach those who do not know. According to Mannheim,

> *"a few persons can see things in a form ever more clear and in an ever widening field, with a result that the capacity of the common man to make rational judgments enters into a gradual and constant decline beginning from the moment when they transfer their responsibility for making decisions to the organization."*[14]

As a final consequence, most individuals become more and more habituated to being directed by others, gradually losing their hold on their own capacity to interpret what is happening around them. This is a basic theme found in the works of William White (*The Organization Man*), of Charles Reich (*The Greening of America*), of Scott and Hart *(The Organizational America)*, of A. Guerreiro Ramos (*The New Science of Organizations*),[15] not to mention Mannheim and other scholars of the Frankfurt School in the decades of the '40s and '50s, who were concerned about the predominance of utilitarian characteristics in our organizational and industrialized society.

Our final observation is that independently of what we might be able to think or say, our industrial civilization has arrived at a crossroads:

a. in the name of efficiency we have been able to standardize thought and action;

---

14. Mannheim, *op. cit.*
15. Wm. H. White, *The Organization Man.* NY: Doubleday Anchor, 1975; Charles A. Reich, *The Greening of America.* NY: Random House, 1970; W. G. Scott and D. Hart, *Organizational America.* Boston: Houghton Mifflin, 1979; and A. Guerreiro Ramos, *The New Science of Organizations.* Toronto: University of Toronto Press, 1982

b. we have developed educational systems for the socialization of people which have as their objective the homogenization of everyone;

c. we have evolved means of communication—the media—capable of forming a uniform set of opinions among the population.

All of these efforts are justified and may even be necessary to the functioning of a society. However, in themselves they are not sufficient.

This imbalance between the substantive and the functional permits us, as a society, to learn how to do some things in a more and more perfect way, but leaves us quite disoriented as to *what* to do according to ethical parameters. Speaking metaphorically, we have the sensation of navigating in a speedy craft, at night, without any instruments of navigation aboard, and without compass or chart. More than discouraging, to the authors, this seems genuinely scary.

2. PARADOXES OF MANAGING

Paradox can only be 'managed' in the sense of coping with, which is what management had always meant until the term was purloined to mean planning and control.

—Charles Handy, *The Age of Paradox.*

Planning the Unplannable

A basic notion flowing out of the rational/scientific paradigm is the idea that since it is believed that we can *predict* and, to some extent, *control* events as they unfold, it is possible to *plan* and to *implement* the future of our lives and of the organizations in which we live and work. A point of view to be developed here is the idea that human relationships are far too idiosyncratic, too individualistic, too subject to unpredicted and unpredictable events, that *planning* in any rational sense is more fantasy than reality when applied to one's personal life.

However, it is safe to affirm that humans are guided by *intentions*—intended actions and outcomes serve as basic motivators as we move through the day and interact with persons and events. Unexpected impediments can arise which thwart an intention, but these are dealt with only as temporary delays in this purposeful motivation to achieve an objective. The concept of *intention* is flexible enough, in relation to common sense coping behavior, that it seems no great matter to modify the objective of the intention if and when the range of possibilities seems to exclude what was originally intended. We shall here sustain the idea that common-sense intentions can give a sense of long-term guidance for the individual operating in a less-than-rational world.

Managing the less-than-rational

All of us like to think that human affairs are essentially rational, and therefor they should be manageable in a rational way, just like other challenges that managers face every day. The great number and variety of personal experiences that negate this "wisdom" never seem to move us to give up the notion, nor to search for better ways of comprehending the world of human relationships.

In an earlier chapter we proposed that the Western-preferred, rational-scientific view of the world we inhabit has been facing serious criticisms as to the reality of its description of lived events. With the introduction of the theories of relativity and quantum mechanics, discoveries about the physical makeup of the atom have threatened our familiar ideas of cause-effect rules, introducing the need for the concept of uncertainty and calling into question long held ideas about the physical world we live in.

Small wonder then that alternative ways of viewing the world should be offered and discussed not only in academia, but also in the workplace and reaching into the daily life of citizens. When former certainty about how things work is replaced by paradox and uncertainty, how shall we continue to see the world with the same eyes? It has been in this context that modern physicists have turned to Eastern mysticism for conceptual insights, and modern youth have turned to existential views of the lived world. They have conceded—

> *that life is absurd, that human affairs usually work not rationally but paradoxically, and that (fortunately) we can never quite master our relationships with others.... certainly true in regard to our relationships in business and other bureaucratic organizations. It is my hope to encourage managers and all those in positions of leadership to think beyond conventional wisdom—in particular, to understand how the ways we think shape what we see, and how paradox and absurdity inevitably play a part in our every action.*[16]

---

16. Richard Farson, *Management of the Absurd: Paradoxes in Leadership.* NY: Simon & Schuster, 1996. p.11

Manage in an Absurd World?

How does one manage in an absurd world? "Managing" has always searched for the most rational, the most efficient (lowest cost, shortest time) way to achieve objectives. But the existential view of the world argues that while much of the physical-object world seems to obey rational rules, such rational rules certainly do not work in the world of human relations. Here the non-rational, the unexpected, the paradoxical, the absurd are usually better descriptors of how things are going.

So how does one "manage" the non-rational, the paradoxical, the absurd? First of all, it is necessary to give up the idea of trying to impose a customary but limited rationality on one's understanding of events. Humans are actually quite adept at dealing with paradox and absurdity—it is just that our preparation as managers has produced in us a "trained incompetence" in dealing with the non-rational in our role as managers.

An Extra-Rational Paradigm?

Actually, it is a matter of the conceptual paradigm in use. We have been taught for years that the technology of management is based upon making *rational* sense out of the hurly-burley that goes on in an office or on a factory floor. We have been taught that if we cannot make it fit into a *rational* framework, we have failed to "see" the problem as professionals are trained to see them, and we are "failures" as managers if we cannot cast the scenario in rationalistic terms.

But because of the way human minds work, inevitably we can see things only as we "intend" to see them. The natural inclination when confronted with absurdities (i.e., non-rational events or situations) is to attempt to "resolve" them by identifying or creating something familiar out of the strange, in order to enable them appear as rational to our trained minds.

Extra-rational talents

However, humans have many other mental talents in addition to rationality, and several of them are invoked when dealing with the absurd. Only we must learn to abandon the habit of *intending* that it is necessary, somehow, to see the *rational* elements in this bizarre situation. Left to everyday modes, humans regularly cope with non-rational situations and events. *"Well, yes and no "* responses to questions are common occurrences, easily handled, and may even be interpreted as a kind of wisdom. The idea that one can have *"too much of a good thing"* is paradoxical, but readily understood without further explanation.

A person appears at the door claiming to be, or to represent, something out of the ordinary, unexpected. There is no rational way to decide whether or not to believe the representation and accede to the request, so we call upon our *intuitions* to help us decide how to respond, with little or no help from the rational. In other words, to cope with the absurd (as in humor) or with the paradoxical (as in "yes and no") is an almost daily occurrence for most people.

But in the work of professional management, to fail to fit a scenario into rational categories and procedures is viewed as either professional incompetence or abandonment of rational purpose. The authors believe that the maturing manager needs to be freed from this rationalistic bias so that he or she is enabled to make use of wider-ranging conceptual abilities of which humans are capable, including intuitive and non-verbalized insights into events and problems.

Coping with absurdity in real life

In a scene from a movie made in the 1930s, *Mr. Smith Goes to Washington,* James Stewart plays a young man just elected to the US Senate. Before leaving to take up this post, he is offered some paradoxical advice from his father: "Lost causes are the only ones worth fighting for." Author Farson explains his understanding of the paradox—lost causes are the ones most worth fighting for because they tend to be the most important, the most humane ones. Lost causes cannot be won, but because they are so crucial in our lives, we nevertheless must try.[17]

He tells the story of a senior scientist in a university agricultural research laboratory who learned to cope with absurdity by being forced periodically to deal with what appeared to be absurd projects dreamed up by colleagues—growing plants in sea water, greening the deserts, and the like. But instead of throwing up his hands in frustration, he chose instead to go ahead as if each were possible, coping with the feeling of absurdity but acting anyway. When questioned about his feelings, he remarked that it is as if he descends into a deep valley (he called it the Valley of the Absurd) until he reaches the peaceful security of the valley floor. Farson writes that in that metaphor the scientist captures the essence of coping with absurdity. Dramatizing a bit, Farson writes:

---

17. Farson, p. 163

I would say that he has (1) allowed the enormity of the situation to wash over him in all its irrationality, (2) embraced the absurdity, even though he could not fully comprehend it, (3) fallen prostrate before its overwhelming complexity, giving up before he starts, and (4) then, calling upon the deep reservoir of will, discipline, experience, creativity, and even playfulness that lies within, picked himself up and started anyway, still respectful, in one corner of his mind, of the fundamental absurdity that he first recognized.[18]

Unpredictable moods

Another unpredictable factor affecting human relationships which is frequently encountered by managers is called "mood swings"—they affect managers as well as individual employees at unpredictable times. I refer to what a writer in the Wall Street Journal calls "the blahs[19]," referring to the "letdown" that often comes after periods of intense work, or as part of one's normal mood cycle. You feel tired and unfocused, unable to tackle even simple tasks.

Unfortunately, daily home and work obligations seldom leave much tolerance for the days when your *joie de vivre* and your ambition are depressed. Especially if you are a manager, despite occasionally feeling "down" you nevertheless are expected to be "up" in your temperament, able to encourage and motivate your employees.

For most of us, a case of the "blahs" lasts only a few days. If you find you cannot pull yourself out of the funk by then, it could be something more serious: job burnout or clinical depression. Before it becomes career-damaging, there are steps you can take to help you shake off the depressed mood, ranging from time away from work to a search for new ways to look at the problem.

The author of the article began by eliminating extraneous issues that were contributing to feeling overwhelmed and incompetent, several of them related to obligations at home or in personal life. Curious about how others handled mood swings, he telephoned several managers to discuss the problem. The managing partner of a New York law firm admitted: *"Any professional or senior manager has periods where they don't want to deal with anything."* This man dealt with such times by diverting himself with projects outside the office. He happened to be an invited board member of several non-profit organizations, and could always find something different and useful he could do for one of their projects. Besides

18.   Farson, p.165
19.   Hal Lancaster, "How to Chase Away the Blahs You Get From Working So Hard," in THE WALL STREET JOURNAL, Vol. CXXXV, No. 36, 20 August 1996, p. B1

breaking up his mental log jam, he also could feel good about donating his efforts to a worthy cause.

Ms. Kaye, executive director of Beverly Kaye & Associates in California, reported that trying to work through the problem of the blahs is a waste of time. For her, *"The best thing is to walk away and get some needed rest, both physically and mentally."* Based upon her own experiences, she took the step of instituting "sick and tired" (S&T) days for her employees. She allows her staff to take up to five days a year to deal with those times when they feel they are in a "funk." If you cannot take an S&T day, she suggests that you ask yourself what most interests you in the workday, and do that. It is important to break the routine and do something spontaneous, she says.

When all else fails, it is good advice to give your colleagues fair warning that you are not up to your normally good mood to minimize damage in your relationships. One manager would wear a "happy face" button upside down to warn her employees that she was not having a "good day" that day. Thus warned, the employees were able to forgive crankiness and lack of focus when the manager was suffering from the blahs.

In summary, like very many human traits and attributes, spontaneous mood swings, mental "highs" and "lows," are unpredictable, as much for managers as for employees. They can be coped with in the same sense that other contingencies can be accommodated. If they were "plannable," of course, we would never include them in tomorrow or next week's calendar!

However, despite these criticisms and clarifications, modern culture's typical way of thinking continues to be as Greek as it was a century ago. The predominant paradigm by which the West interprets the world is, without doubt, the Aristotelian: rational, planned. And if personally we operate in such a manner, well and good, since at least to act in a "logical and rational" manner is effectively in accord with the parameters of the current societal paradigm.

In this rational form, for the reasons already discussed, we intend to outline the fundamentals of a model for your own *personal planning.* It was elaborated some time ago, in an epoch in which, at least for the authors, there was a steadfast faith in the possibility of a *planned life.* Undeniably this was useful during a certain stage of our lives. Who knows if it may not be useful for you as well, dear reader?

Nevertheless, an alerting is in order: if you opt for this route—that of searching for greater security and foresight via rational, personal planning—do not forget the words of counsel from Whitehead: *"The aim of science is to seek the simplest explanations of complex facts...Seek simplicity and distrust it."*[20]

3. Individual Planning: How To Improve Your Capacity And Impact

A majority of the people with whom we share this organizational society agree with the idea that we live in a turbulent environment. However, the conclusion usually drawn from this is often erroneous, the idea that *we cannot explain either how nor why we should attempt to plan in such an environment, when modifications are occurring at an accelerated rate.* This conclusion derives from a wrongly held conception about the legitimate function of planning. Interpreting it as "seeing the future" has been a constant mistake. Those who have seen already that such a function is an impossibility—because it is clear that none of us possesses a crystal ball—we propose to reconceptualize individual planning, beginning with a new point of view: the idea of *planning as a construction of the future.* It is a cerebral activity, thought through, structured, contributing to the realization of one's own personal intentions.

What you will find in the following section deals with a process of reflection about the critical elements considered important to your individual planning.

Individual Planning (IP)

According to Donald H. Swartz, Individual Planning (IP) is a process that permits a person to clarify values, identify needs and desires, and establish objectives in vital terms, within a frame of reference of organizational and environmental expectations that are extremely changeable.[21]

IP does not cease to be microplanning if compared to organizational planning (OP), which makes use of such methods as interpersonal and intergroup learning, associating them with techniques of planning from administrative sciences. To recognize the problems of IP does not affirm that such planning should not be elaborated. All of us do it, in one form or another. There is, however, an enormous difference between doing it in an experimental, non-systematic way, and doing it according to certain orientations and guidelines pre-established. The intention here is to present a model within which the elements judged necessary

---

20.   Alfred North Whitehead, *The Aims of Education.* NY: Mentor Books, 1929
21.   Donald H. Swartz, "Life Goals Planning for Managers," in Taylor, Bernard and Lippitt, Gordon L., eds. *Management Development and Training Handbook.* Maidenhead Berkshire, England: McGraw-Hill, 1975. p.342

to individual planning are marked out and established. Beginning with the model, it is possible to structure an entire methodology by which to operationalize the important elements of individual planning.

The model as conceived (see **Figure 7.1**) implies the existence of an individual, with his or her desires and needs. The model seeks to clarify personal values, whether considered relevant or irrelevant. Beginning with this, the next step is to establish one's personal objectives and plan ways to achieve them. Individual planning is elaborated while taking into account that one is a member of some organization, itself inevitably subject to change, and which is also a part of a wider system called the organizational ecology.

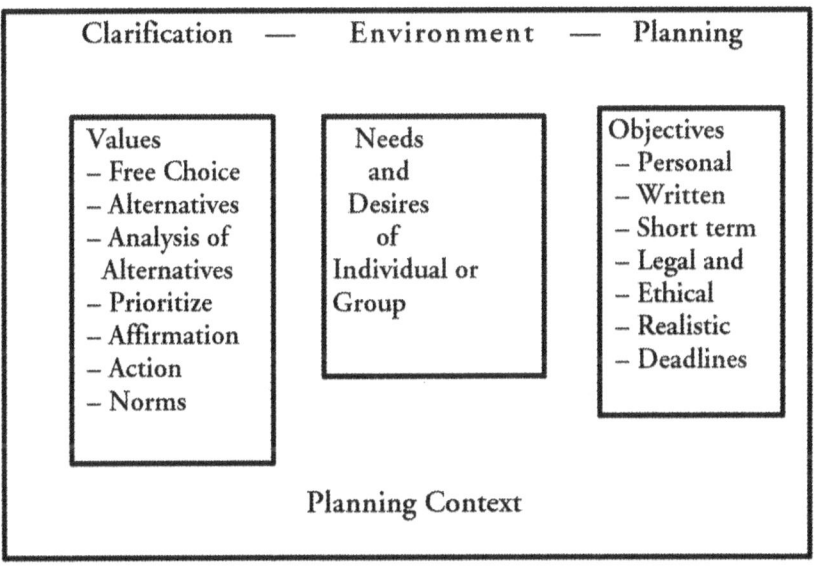

Figure 7.1 Individual Planning
Organizational Ecology

Advantages of Individual Planning

If we desire that individuals acquire or improve habits of personal planning, it is important that they see some concrete advantage from such an activity. Therefore, we have proposed a series of topics for reflection, as justifications for doing individual planning. Without being convinced of its value, with all certainty no consequent action will flow from it. The topics mentioned are those that follow:

—An opportunity to create a future and to plan its realization

—While some permit their lives to move on, day by day, others work to give direction or sense to their lives. Molding the future is considered a value judged valid to pursue.

—When so many are oriented toward their past, there is a special value to be found when individuals attempt to orient their existence in future terms, a future that is at least partially planned.

—Individual planning moves us toward dedicating time to reflect on a complex of personal objectives, and at the same time to establish priorities between what is considered simply *important* from what is actually *essential.* According to Drucker, that which is considered *essential* will get done. The rest will tend to fall by the wayside.

—Individual planning is intimately linked with the concept of organizational planning, except that now the objectives are those of the individual and not of the organization. To transfer the notion of individual planning to organizational planning is a simple and natural process.

—Professional planning, that is, planning which relates the activities of individuals more closely to organizational objectives, can better be done within the life planning of the individual.

—When the individual has greater clarity in relation to the plans for their life, they will generally find a better sense of self-acceptance; a new sense of personal liberty; a recognition of their individual potential; a better appreciation of the importance of themselves to their organization; a higher motivation to establish objectives and to achieve them; and a better disposition toward participation in organizational planning.

—The inclusion of individual planning as part of organizational planning demonstrates a social concern extremely positive on the part of the organization, and reflects a growing tendency which we believe will characterize future years: greater participation and greater integration between individual and organization.

Individual planning offers the following advantages:[22]

For the Individual:

—The recognition of one's personal potential and a renewed sense of self-confidence.

—The opportunity to articulate one's work objectives with one's personal objectives and to methodically plan how to achieve them.

—*Insight* to develop a greater initiative and motivation in oneself as well as in others.

—A more objective view of one's image and of the image that one projects to others.

—The means to prepare oneself psychologically for more satisfactory relations with family and associates.

—A clearer vision of interpersonal relationships between spouses, opening new ways of communication and comprehension.

—The opportunity to define mutual objectives that can be shared with spouse.

—Becoming aware in a clearer way of the expectations, objectives, problems, and aspirations of one's companion.

For the Organization

—The development of a greater balance and better harmony, in the home as well as in the place of work.

—The means to increase initiative and motivation of individuals to establish objectives and to achieve them.

—The strengthening of psychological bonds between individual and organization.

—A greater readiness on the part of the individual to participate in organizational planning.

---

22. George Ford, *et al., Personal Planning Workbook,* 2nd edition. WDC: Mid-Atlantic Training Committee, 1973. pp. 1-2

—The means of giving leaders a heightened vision of the importance of change, as much for the leader as for the organization.

—The means to give the individual a greater consciousness of one's potential and a way of making it more effective.

—The opportunity for the individual to understand him/herself better, and thus to better understand others with whom one must communicate.

—Individuals better elaborate their individual planning in the light of clearly understood organizational objectives.

Individual Planning Model

Clarification of values—In order for something to be considered a value, the following seven prerequisites need to be satisfied. Collectively, these also describe the *process* of the clarification of values.

1. Freedom to choose: Regardless of whether some authority figure is observing and controlling, anything that gives orientation to one's life should be the product of one's own free will.

2. Choice among alternatives: There cannot be choice if there are no alternatives among which to choose. Only when there exists more than one alternative, can there be expressed some valued choice.

3. Characteristics of the choice: Choices made impulsively and without serious reflection do not move us toward long-term values. If something can orient the life of an individual in an intelligent and significant way, that something should emerge from being understood, weighed, and evaluated from among available alternatives.

4. Appreciation: When one values something, it is esteemed and respected, and one usually remains content with these values. But it is also possible to express a free and thoughtful choice, yet not be happy with the decision: you may decide to participate in a struggle, but remain unhappy with the conditions which made such a choice the most reasonable.

5. Public affirmation: when you choose something freely, after having considered the alternatives, and when you are proud of this choice, you are prepared to publicly affirm these values.

6. Reflection on the action: a value tends to make itself visible in people's lives. If something is valued, the person gives time, money, and talents to that which has been elected as a value. There is no doubt that time and energy will be found to give to what these values represent. You cannot consider something a value which does not give some direction to one's life. Persons who talk a good deal about something but take no action in relation to it, with all certainty are not wrestling with values.

7. Repetition: there is a repeated appearance of the value in some norm of behavior. When something has value for us, it tends to reappear in people's lives in different times and different situations. Something that is observed once, and never seen again, cannot be considered a value. Values are persistent. They become norms that are incorporated into one's life.

Collectively these seven criteria delineate the *valorative process*. It is inevitably associated with an individual's choices and actions. The results of this process we call *values*. We want to emphasize that this valorative process has as its consequence the action of *values formation*. This is because the entire methodology of individual planning tries to emphasize the idea that values are dynamic and changeable, and that they will change along the continuum of one's life. Sydney Simon writes, *"…certain things are seen as certain, desirable. These tend to become values for the individual."*[23] Humans, who are dynamic beings, will value different things in different ways, and possibly the same things in a modified form at different times in one's life.

Thus in this first phase, individual planning has as its objectives:

a. It gives the individual a methodology that permits the person, in a systematic and disciplined way, to clarify his/her values;

b. It carries the individual to an identification of his/her present values, and to an acceptance of the changeableness of personal values. This is somewhat contrary to traditional education, that defines values as immutable norms;

c. It positions the individual as a member of one or more organizations, each situated in a wider social context.

The orientation to establish personal objectives—These are only the orienting criteria, having much in common with aspects of the formulation of organizational objectives.

Personal ownership—There is a greater probability that the individual will attain personally established objectives than objectives established by others. This does not mean that an individual will not recognize objectives expressed by a

---

23. Sydney B. Simon, *et al.*, "Values and teaching," s.1, Charles E. Merrill Books, 1966. Cited by George Ford in his *Personal Planning Workbook, op. cit,* p. 24

spouse, a friend, or a boss as shared objectives. These can be accepted, but motivation will be greater when the advantages and disadvantages of working toward a determined objective are consciously weighed, and a personal decision is made to pursue it.

Objectives must be written—The fact of writing down what is proposed achieves a double function:

—It clarifies for the individual himself what he really wants to do, permitting conscious revisions and modifications;

—It requires a greater involvement and effort that also generates a greater commitment and sense of responsibility in achieving stated objectives.

Short-term objectives—One should initially establish objectives that are not too ambitious, ones that can be achieved in a relatively short time period. With this, one has the possibility of gaining greater self-confidence in one's own efforts. Before you can run, it is necessary to learn to walk.

Legality and ethics—Before making a decision to pursue seriously some objective that might possibly conflict with personal values, or with the existing norms of the society at a given time, it will be worthwhile to attempt to answer, for yourself, some questions: Is this objective considered legal in my society? In case it is *not*, am I disposed to pay the price society will impose if I am caught in it? Is this objective in agreement with my personal values?

Realism—An objective which, *a priori,* you know to be impossible to achieve, in fact is not an objective, but only a dream. To affirm that an objective must be realistic does not signify that it must be unpretentious or audacious, but only that it be a reasonable one, that can motivate the individual to pursue it, and simultaneously, that one has the strength and energy to achieve it. Only you, individually, will be able to decide whether or not a given objective will actually be attained.

Deadlines—Fixing deadlines and dates for completion of objectives is part of one's own nature. There is a profound difference between the two following affirmations:

—I will dedicate four nights per week to the family.

—I will dedicate four nights per week to the family, beginning on January 1, 2005.

In the first case, the required action can be postponed indefinitely. In the second, one must gather one's psychological energies to take the necessary concrete steps, and beginning with a specific date, cease to teach evening classes at the university and remain at the house with the wife and family (as a simple example).

Criticisms of Individual Planning

The criticisms normally made of the notion of clarification of individual objectives is that in a society—including the global as well as organizational society—where predominant values are *bad-faith, exploitation and distrust*, he who does not hide his aspirations, who affirms clearly his objectives, may be at a disadvantage.

The counter-criticism that one can make is to first *call into doubt the idea that bad faith, exploitation, distrust, and competition* are in fact the dominant values in all societies. If in fact these supposedly dominant values are accepted as a given, then everyone's behavior should conform to them and suffer their results: non-shared objectives, low participation, extremely defensive behaviors, constant competition, and denial or negation of willing collaboration.

If this be the case, one can apply with every justification, Douglas McGregor's concept of a *self-fulfilling prophecy*. In other words, if we adopt these assumptions (in this case, bad faith, exploitation, etc.), which have not been tested, or that may have emerged from a single or unique personal experience, we will end up creating a society made uncivil by our own worst nightmares.

Because there are negative personal experiences, or stories of such experiences, we too often find more exploitation than encouragement, more bad faith and competition than good faith and collaboration. People learn to hide their personal motives and objectives. Such behavior ends up being cultivated in every context, even in those where it is considered improper or inappropriate. It is necessary for people to be clear about what their objectives are, and that they learn how to distinguish among situations where they can safely share personal feelings, and other situations where they should be more reserved. Choose rather to encourage, in the final analysis, a behavior which is conscious, pragmatic, variable according to the situation, and not an undifferentiated behavior unrelated to the situation, context, and culture.

Conclusions

We said initially that we have not intended to provide specific techniques for achieving Individual Planning, but only to mark its importance. Our assumption is that if individual planning is done, based upon a vision not merely functionalist, but also including substantive values, it will possess the conditions with which to contribute as much to the ordering the personal life of the individual as for the society in which we live and move. As for the rest, we point out that if one has an individual plan, it becomes easier to make it compatible with the organizational plan. Here the words of Seneca seem appropriate: *"There is no favorable wind for those who do not know where they are going."*

4. LEARNING TO LEARN

Learning is perhaps the most natural thing that humans do. Babies are constantly seeking out and testing new modes of action and re-action in the family group, and the baby that does not actively learn in this way becomes an immediate concern to mother and father. The newborn does not need to "learn to learn"—rather, active learning is the most natural thing a healthy child does. Its inquisitive search for new learning becomes a mark of its intelligence, and its exploration of context and capabilities a guarantee that the child is normal in its development and growth.

Why, then, as adults do we become concerned about learning how to learn? Because somewhere along the way to adulthood, while acquiring a great deal of knowledge, we have also acquired habits and limitations to the learning process. In adults, spontaneous learning comes to be replaced by habit and routine, by deeply held ideologies and cultural values, tunnel vision, selective perception, and deference to the judgments of others.[24] These all become the enemies in our efforts to see, to understand, to learn what is really going on. Spontaneous learning has changed from a natural curiosity about what is going on about us to a task or chore imposed by parents, teachers and employers.

So, paradoxically, our capacity to learn includes some qualities which tend to teach us to stop learning. Our every success in learning creates impediments to continued learning. Because of what modern youth might call the *"been there, done that"* syndrome, once we have learned an acceptable way to handle a situation, we seldom question further whether or not we might learn to improve it. Once a successful response to a problem or event has been archived in memory and habit, it is only with reluctance that we will return to reconsider it. We continue to operate sub-optimally, based upon unexamined responses developed into habits from earlier experiences.

---

24.   Richard Farson, *Management of the Absurd: Paradoxes in Leadership.* NY: Simon & Schuster, 1996. p. 28

A Very Helpful Personal Robot

Author Colin Wilson tells a parable about an imaginary robot that illustrates the point very well. As a young man, Wilson needed to learn to use the typewriter. He bought a typewriter and an instruction book, and began the tedious process of teaching himself to type. At first, he says, he had to think carefully about the precise movements each finger had to make to strike a key and produce an image on the paper. But slowly, his friendly mental robot began to learn the necessary maneuvers, and after a time, Wilson noted that it was only necessary to think of a word or phrase he wanted to write, and presto! the helpful robot typed it almost effortlessly on the paper.

The robot turned out to be similarly useful when he began to learn to drive an automobile. At first, Wilson had to give detailed attention to every movement necessary to control the automobile's speed and trajectory, but after the robot learned the necessary routines, it was possible to carry on a serious conversation with passengers while at the same time effortlessly driving in traffic. The robot also learned, over time, to serve as an English/French interpreter when Wilson traveled to France to study. A very useful robot, indeed.

But in due time Wilson began to observe some disadvantages associated with his personal robot's assistance. He writes that he loved classical music, but he began to notice that after hearing an orchestral piece three or four times, his mental robot began to take over his spontaneous enjoyment of its nuances, as though to say, "I've already learned this one—you can do something else while I take care of it." A similar occurrence as he watched a series of splendid sunsets from his patio. In a moment of pique, Wilson exclaims, "I've even caught that darned robot making love to my wife!"

Wilson's parable serves to illustrate how successful patterns of learning become habituated and thus become impediments to further learning. So we conclude that when, as adults, we talk about "learning to learn" we are really talking about learning to *unlearn*—how to unlearn many useful and successful habits we have built up over the years which unwittingly block the spirit and practice of really *new* learning.

> *Without quite knowing it, we have become creatures of linear, categorical logic. Things are good or bad, true or false, but not both. We have been taught that a thing cannot be what it is and also its opposite. Yet it sounds wise when confronted with a conflict to say, "Well, yes and no."*[25]

Adult Learning Begins With Un-learning

Implementing change, personal or organizational, will involve un-learning some tried-and-true habits in order to learn new, and more appropriate, actions. Farson observes the paradox that the healthier you are psychologically, the less you may seem to *need* change, but the easier it will be for you to actually change.[26] In other words, the healthier you are psychologically, the easier it is to un-learn old habits in order to learn new and better ones.

Some of the elements of adult "learning to learn"

A willingness to experience and explore new ways of "seeing" physical, cultural, and moral aspects of the world. In **Part I** we illustrated the advantages of "paradigm competence," of possessing several different paradigmatic modes of understanding events. The content of paradigms includes families of assumptions we take for granted about physical and emotional things that touch us. Learning new ways to cope with your world and its problems will involve un-learning some habits and values which you have held for years, to find them replaced by other logics based upon a different set of assumptions. By the same token, un-learning old habits will probably involve abandonment of long-preferred ways of doing things, of conducting your personal business.

  A conscious expansion of your personal horizons. This might include:

a.   **a return to the study** of something not associated with your professional life, such as joining a club associated with a hobby or avocation, one which provides occasions for new friends and new learning.

b.   **wide reading;** history, philosophy, anthropology, biographical studies of leaders, historical fiction, technical journals.

c.   **travel,** learning a language, broadening your views of the world by "seeing" through the eyes of other cultures.

---

25.   Richard Farson, *Management of the Absurd: Paradoxes in Leadership.* NY: Simon & Schuster, 1996. p. 21
26.   Farson, Management of the Absurd. p. 85

Keep a personal journal

Keeping a journal is a means to learn systematically from personal experience. It provides a low-cost means of noting and analyzing events, in reflecting on their meaning, and as a stimulus to think about alternative ways to understand them.

As youths[27] both authors were fascinated with flying, and aspired to be pilots some day. As young men both took flying lessons and earned a pilot's license. During that period we subscribed to a magazine called *Flying*, and a favorite monthly section was entitled *"I Learned About Flying From That..."* This was inevitably a 2-3 page story told by pilots taken from personal accounts of emergencies or near-accidents which usually stemmed from reliance on habits or presumptions ingrained into the pilot's practices over years of flying. But in the case recounted in the story, the habitual practice either contributed directly to the emergency, or failed to be sufficient to the problem. So the ending of each story specified what old thing the pilot had *un-learned,* and what new thing he had *learned* about safe flying from that emergency experience.

In recommending the use of a personal journal, the authors see many concrete advantages for the interested learner. First of all, choosing what to write and writing it on the page tends to fix it in the memory, leading to more accurate and easier recall.

Secondly, returning to read and to reflect on what has been written after a few days (or weeks) tends to put into comparative perspective the issues which have been matters of concern or satisfaction. (There will be satisfaction of seeing how some situations which were a source of deep concern came to be resolved, along with hints about whether and/or how it might have been more easily or better handled.)

Thirdly, a few months of journal records will begin to reveal glimpses of your own, personal administrative theory, applied by you in the practice of your work. Fourthly, a few months of journal records will identify both long-term problems as well as long-term trends in the development of your organization and of your own career.

Deliberately interrupt personal, habituated routines in order to experiment with new modes, new ideas. As adults (males especially) we develop and cling to routines for "safeness" in our personal relationships and ourselves. Social rules seem to conspire to reward routine in our relationships one with another, in the interests of predictability.

---

27.   Both authors are licensed civilian pilots, with a good amount of hours logged in the pilot's seat.

But this routinization of daily life can be the enemy of new learning. Comfortable though it may be, it is the comfort of stagnation, of stalled development. Sometimes it is useful to deliberately change one's eating or sleeping habits, simply to break up the routine; to change habits of leisure, to develop deliberately a new vision of one's *persona* or role(s) in relation to friends and ourselves. Women seem to enjoy such changes—a new hair color, different dress styles, different restaurants, and different clubs.

Heuristic learning

This is the most exciting of all. *"Heuristic"* comes from a Greek root meaning *"to discover,"* and it characterizes the rush of excitement felt by child and adult alike when they "discover" the secret behind some puzzling fact or behavior.

Infants practice **heuristic learning** every waking moment. Heuristically, they learn how to roll over, to sit up, to feed themselves, to control their parents and fight with their siblings. Heuristically they learn to understand language and to speak, and in the process, they learn to communicate with other living beings. For them, every day is a spontaneous and marvelous journey of discovery of what is new, what is possible, and what may be [temporarily] impossible.

Childhood learning in elementary school is usually labeled **memorization or rote learning**, the tedious memorization of addition and multiplication tables, of rules of spelling, grammar and syntax, of historical dates and geographical place-names. This is the kind of learning that effectively turns off the spontaneity in knowledge acquisition, even while there is no substitute for it in Western culture. This basic knowledge store, laid down in memory by arduous and boring repetition, becomes the key to more advanced knowledge at higher levels of education.

Most adult learning is **associative**—that is, new learning occurs through the association of fact or experience with something learned earlier, and already archived in the memory. Hence, it can be argued that adults seldom experience really new learning, rather, there is simply the formation of an associative connection between daily experiences and related knowledge categories already existing in memory. This being the case, it becomes important to "seed" the mind with new frameworks, new ideas, new knowledge categories to which new learning can be "hooked" in an associative way.

Relation between rationality and intuition in "learning to learn."

As we have repeatedly suggested throughout this section, our "scientific" culture has over-emphasized the rational component of human intelligence. Since infancy, we have been taught to discount or to control emotional or intuitive responses to events in favor of rationally derived techniques as "preferred" interactive behavior.

We are suggesting here that human intelligence includes more than rationality, that we have innate capacities to "see" and to respond intuitively to the ambiguity and paradox of day-to-day problems that is wider ranging and more comprehensive than we have been taught to believe.

In Western culture there are conditionings that form part of early training which teach us *not* to respond to emotions or intuitive feelings arising from real or imagined threats to our sense of well being. My mother taught me time and time again not to act if I was feeling anger or annoyance. Rather, she taught me to count to ten, slowly, before getting involved in a hasty action which might escalate the problem, or that I might later regret.

This is good early-childhood training, but reinforced through a lifetime of trained repression to intuitive responses, adult perceptive skills eventually become severely limited and we ultimately fail to "see" other than those trained, habituated responses to new problems which arise in new contexts. We believe that modern managers need to be able to employ all the capabilities in the human cognitive armarium to function innovatively in today's rapidly changing technological and economic environments.

Managerial Training vs. Education

As we know, managerial training can lead to the development of skills and techniques. Each new technique implicitly reinvents the manager's job with a new definition of the task, a new burden of responsibility because it increases the area of control for which managers feel responsible.

For example, if we teach a manager techniques for dealing with employees troubled by drug use, or with emotional problems, that manager will probably feel more responsible for the well being of those employees—his or her area of responsibility has been enlarged. But because techniques don't work well in human relations, the manager is often unable to resolve adequately such problems, creating a dangerous combination of feelings of inadequacy. Experience teaches that in human relations, responsibility plus helplessness leads to confrontation, argument, and insult, even abuse. So we conclude that management development based upon training in techniques will never be sufficient to meet the challenges of executive development.

Management Education

Education, on the other hand, leads not to technique but to information and knowledge, which in the right hands can lead to insight and understanding, even to wisdom. And wisdom leads to humility, compassion, and respect—qualities that are fundamental to effective leadership.[28]

Farson writes that training makes people more alike, because everyone learns the same skills. Education, because it involves relating one's personal ideas in the light of great ideas, tends to make people different from each other. So the first benefit of education is that the manager becomes unique, independent, authentic. And with education comes a better understanding of the context in which one's decisions are imbedded, a better perspective for viewing human affairs, and a better idea of what is truly important. This can lead to vision, another quality of leadership that characterizes top executives.[29]

Becoming more efficient learners

How can we become more efficient learners? Earlier we have emphasized the importance of paradigm competence, of acquiring several different ways to view the world. Then we discussed that adult learning is **associative learning**—new learning happens when we are able to associate new experience and new ideas with concepts and ideas already a part of our personal repertoire. This argues that learning to learn involves deliberately expanding the vocabulary of our personal conceptual repertoire by reading and learning about entirely new things, in areas that are new to us.

Are they introducing computers into your organization, and you are computer illiterate? It's time to begin to read about the origins and development of this important technology. These authors believe that simple training at the keyboard, the mechanistic acquisition of keystrokes to do certain things, will never satisfy a manager's need to be computer literate. Background reading into the

---

28. Farson, p.155
29. Farson, p. 155

development of solid state electronics and binary logic systems will lead to a much richer understanding of what happens when you touch the keyboard. As managers, you will need to make decisions about the acquisition of computers and software in your workplace, and if you are limited to a few hours of use-training for one or two software programs, your counsel will be seriously limited by your lack of experience and general knowledge.

Professional vs. Amateur

Do you have an avocation, a hobby, which you pursue with some passion? Farson writes that the good leader must be both professional and amateur. The Latin root for the French word *amateur* comes from *amator*, meaning "lover." So the French used the word *amateur* to designate people who pursue some avocation out of passion, or love, rather than for monetary gain. Love is fundamental to good leadership, because leadership is all about caring, and caring is the basis for building a sense of community, a sincere feeling of unity, of fellowship with others.[30]

In the case of managers, the good leader must be both a professional and an amateur.

> *The professional conforms to technical and ethical standards which require a high level of proficiency based on sound knowledge and conscientiousness. But the amateur performs work out of love, out of the sensuous pleasure in the act of accomplishment, in the creation of community, in the bonds of compassion that unite.*[31]

A passion for learning is a decided advantage for the maturing manager. On the job, he constantly has an open mind to learn from employees and others how better to organize the context and the tasks. Off the job, the passion is to learn something new every day, to keep the juices of personal development flowing. There is an excitement to being alive and being able to learn. We urge you to make it a core characteristic of your being.

---

30. Farson, p. 158
31. Farson, p. 159

Chapter 8:
Managing the Unconscious

Civilized life today demands concentrated, directed conscious functioning,
and this entails the risk of a considerable dissociation from the unconscious.
The further we are able to remove ourselves from the unconscious through
directed functioning, the more readily a powerful counter-position can build
up in the unconscious, and when this breaks out it may have disagreeable
consequences.

—Carl Jung, *The Structure and Dynamics of the Psyche.*

1. MANAGING STRESS

What you will find in this section:

The Nature of Managerial Stress

Physiology of the Stress Reaction

Role of the Unconscious Mind in Stress Management

Introduction

Stress as a Societal Problem

The magazine THE ECONOMIST, in its July 27, 1996 edition, carried a small article entitled *The American Way of Death*. Some items in this article attracted our
attention, because they seem provocative.

According to updated data from the National Center for Health Statistics, the
causes of death in 1997 in the United States can be seen in the following data:

Causes	% Total Deaths
Diseases of the heart	31.4%
Cancers	23.3%
Cerebrovascular diseases	6.9%
Chronic pulmonary diseases	4.7%
Accidents and adverse effects	4.1%
Pneumonia and influenza	3.7%
Diabetes	2.7%

Source: National Vital Statistics Reports, Vol.47, No.19, June 30, 1999

What attracted our immediate attention is that death by cancer, heart and cerebrovascular diseases represent more than sixty percent of the major causes listed above. There is mounting evidence that *stress* is an underlying causative agent of the first three categories, i.e., cancer, heart and cerebrovascular diseases. Without doubt, this is a theme reaching beyond the area of immediate concern of any single medical or professional specialization because it can relate to all of us equally.

Furthermore, there is much evidence that managerial stress represents a multi-billion-dollar problem, with a strong impact in all modern societies. David Tarrant, writing for the Dallas Morning News,[1] reports that modern firms are getting pressure to "rein in" managerial tyrants who regularly "bully" employees under their responsibility. As an example, Tarrant recounts the story of a secretary employed during eight years in a regional office of a federal agency. It was a nice job except for one problem: her boss was an "absolute monster." He routinely screamed and cursed at her. She couldn't quit because her husband did contract work and her $36,000-a-year salary was their only secure income; they also needed the health insurance benefits.

Finally, she got a transfer within the agency, after which she was treated for post-traumatic stress disorder and anxiety attacks. A complaint she filed resulted in an internal investigation, but the supervisor kept his position. She explained: "He gets the job done fastest for the least amount of money. He makes his supe-

---

1.   Reprinted in THE SACRAMENTO BEE, Monday, August 7, 2000 Section C, Business. pp. 1,3

riors in Washington look good." So instead of forcing an end to this manager's tyranny, his supervisors "turn their heads and look the other way."

The reporter writes that these managerial bullies have one thing in common: they consider the workplace a jungle and employees their prey. Many businesses are coming under pressure to tame them. Dr. Loraleigh Keashly, a social psychologist at Wayne State University in Detroit, comments "We spend more time at work than with our families. How we are treated there is very important."

The tough, intimidating boss has always been an icon of American business culture. The problem is aggravated in the current atmosphere of corporate downsizing and mergers. Traditional bonds of loyalty are frayed, anxiety flourishes, and workers feel pitted against each other during rounds of job cutbacks. "Your gain will be at someone else's expense. It's a very hostile world, said Dr. Gary Namie, a California psychologist.[2]

These are not isolated incidents, researchers say. A recent survey of 930 employees in Michigan showed that one in five reported being "significantly mistreated" in the past year. Psychologist Keashly rejects the suggestion that people are being too sensitive with the question: "Is 20 percent of the working population too sensitive?"

As for the people working as managers, Keashly says that managerial bullies are not always the psychopathological monsters they are popularly portrayed to be. Bullying can be a manager's response to extreme stress and frustration, or to the lack of supervisory skills. "Many people move up in the organization, but they are never trained how to supervise. The irony is that most of the "bullies" who come to such supervisory training are good people at heart. They have just learned a lousy way to manage."

Dealing with Managerial Stress

Do you know an intolerant, inflexible and rancorous manager? Have you seen managers who feel threatened, who shout, offend and recriminate subordinates and colleagues in an aggressive way?

If so, you are observing a manager who is suffering from stress! Managerial stress,[3] because of its deleterious impact, and because of how it can be ameliorated using self-hypnosis or professionally assisted therapeutic hypnosis is our next topic of analysis and discussion.

—Why are managers vulnerable to occupational stress?

---

2.   Dr. Namie and his wife have written "The Bully At Work" (*Sourcebooks*, $14.95)

—Is occupational stress always negative?

—What do specialists say about stress?

—Can stress be avoided? How?

—What can hypnosis and visualization do about stress?

We will deal with these questions in the following sections.

The Stress Syndrome

The illness called stress has grown in uninterrupted form and with consequences ever more serious. Stress is presented as a complex picture of symptoms that a majority of medical practitioners are not prepared to diagnose. Diagnosis usually depends upon analysis by a multidisciplinary team, or of specialists experienced in the field.

The symptoms can be confusing because they can range from minor feelings of indisposition to death, from headaches to heart attacks, from indigestion to collapse, from fatigue and elevated blood pressure to hepatitis and hemorrhagic ulcers.

Stress is not an illness transmitted by bacteria or any microorganism. The causes are related to the unconscious controls of physiological functions originating in the brain. Natural desires to feel safe and competent give rise to anxieties when a person feels psychological threatened by circumstances such as when a manager approaches with a negative evaluation. These anxieties, in turn, produce physiological changes triggered by the brain preparing the body for real or imaginary fight or flight responses. These usually include a flood of adrenaline into the system that results in increased heartbeat and blood pressure, tensed muscles, paused digestion or perhaps an acid flux into the stomach. All of this results in a feeling of uncomfortable stress in the employee.

Stress specialists, including Selye, Albrecht, Coleman, Dienstfrey, Arroba, Kasareck, and Rossi affirm that an environment contributing to apprehensiveness, conflict, life-changes for the person, rapid and inexorable change, and pres-

---

3. The material in the following section draws heavily from *"O Stress do Gerente,"* a study paper elaborated jointly by Professor Caravantes and psychologist Marina Keiko Nakayama, while in the course of her doctoral studies in the post-graduate program in administration at the Federal University of the State of Rio Grande do Sul.

sures of work are the usual causes of a feeling of lack of control to which human beings are increasingly exposed.

The environment most favorable to these types of situations is found in organizations. And the persons who are most exposed to stress are the managers, because the functions of the manager involve situations which favor the development of stress.

The manager generally has intensive contact with other people. This contact is not always agreeable because it involves people who are distrustful, unmotivated, competitive, egocentric, insecure, and demanding. The manager's rôle is to establish a certain harmony among conflicting personalities and to create a climate of cooperation in his team. The manager has the function of defining objectives and to organize employees around these objectives, to resolve conflicts, and to make decisions, to wrestle with frustrations, while permanently running risks of error.

To manage persons is a very difficult task. It demands a high level of maturity and personal equilibrium, along with a profound understanding of human nature. And even when gifted with such qualities, the manager can be, and is often, swept along and worn down because of changes that constantly occur in the organizational and social environment:

—The increasing complexity of organizations related to new technologies, internationalization, recessions, and changes in values.

—This increase in organizational complexities can require the need to constantly redefine tasks, to redistribute or reduce the number of personnel, implicating the possible dismissal of some.

—A more competitive market demanding the creation of new products, innovation in terms of services and more efficient modes of marketing.

—Employees are increasingly demanding their "rights," associated perhaps with the demands of the consumer market, price inflation, greater participation, reduction of social distance between manager and subordinate.

—There is an ever larger number of women in the work force, and as a consequence, men have less moral support in the home, while women bear a redoubled responsibility.

—The family no longer plays the same supporting role. The number of children diminishes, but their period of dependency on parental support increases, a function of the need for more schooling in a competitive labor market. There is a reduced amount of "quality time" spent in the home—(electronic games, more liberal rules guiding relationships among young people, access to information from sources external to the family, parents spending more time at work).

The responsibility of managers is greater because this stress, caused by a feeling of loss of control, affects widening numbers of people, compromises the productivity of the organization and adds to his own discomforts.

It is clear that we do not have control over most of the factors that contribute to the mental wear and tear that predisposes to stress. However, there are measures that can reduce the impact of these changes on people.

Why is stress a problem for organizations?

For the individual, stress can provoke discomfort, illness, or even premature death. For the organization, it can mean weak job performance, inefficiency and ineffectiveness.

Although we do not have national or international statistics on the indices of stress of workers and managers, we can give a single example drawn from Porto Alegre, in southern Brazil. There the Chief of Gastroenterological Services at the Clinical Hospital reported that an estimated 50% of those who appear for consultation do not present evidence of any organic illness, but suffer rather from functional disturbances originating from psychological wear and tear in the work place.

According to this Medical Services Chief, about 50 persons daily come to request medical attention in his sector alone, of whom only half present functional disturbances. If the consulting physician is experienced with the symptoms of stress, he can detect problems of stress during the consult, and direct the patient to a psychologist, or perhaps develop a treatment program drawing on different sections of the hospital according to the need. Lacking this, the patient finds himself submitted to a series of laboratory tests and continues to present various symptoms without being cured. All of this increases the overall cost of treatment, without even mentioning the prejudice to the workplace.

The Chief of the third largest cardiology clinic of Brazil, the Heart Institute of Porto Alegre, affirms that any factor that promotes anxiety and stress is a complication for those with heart problems. From January to October of 1992 the Institute treated 77,000 ambulatory cases, 7,300 hospitalizations, and 1,418 surgeries. (These data were provided by the Chief of the Gastroenterological Services of the

Clinical Hospital, which is responsible for the research section of the Heart Institute.)

According to Possas,[4] cardiovascular illnesses have been identified as a major cause of death in Brazil. In 1930 it was responsible for 11.8% of deaths in the country, increasing to 25.8% in 1984, corresponding to 1/3 of the deaths in the Southern and Southeastern regions.

Anna Maria Rossi, Ph.D. in psychology, journalist who writes about this topic in a Porto Alegre newspaper, author of two books on stress, affirms that 80% of visits to medical offices stem from symptoms originating in stress, and that stress can kill, just as does any high risk illness.

Stress plays a decisive and integrative role in every undertaking and every negotiation in the enterprise. Like hereditary factors, foods with a high fat content, and lack of exercise, stress can contribute to cardiac and coronary illnesses, to peptic ulcers, to suicides, nervous disorders, migraine, insomnia, abuse of tranquilizers, drinking problems, conjugal conflicts, allergies, strikes, picketing and violence in the workplace. The causes of these losses for enterprise and industry are immediately visible in the stock market. Some indirect consequences are market downturns, economic crises, political imbalance, and the loss of national identity. We see an enormous drain on vital human resources.[5]

Why are Managers Subject to Negative Stressors?

According to Drucker,[6] an important role of the professional administrator is the managerial function. The managerial function is characterized, according to Drucker, as being responsible for making human resources productive; to get people to work together; to unite their capabilities and knowledge toward a common goal; to exemplify the task of making positive qualities productive and the deficiencies irrelevant. This, in final analysis, is the most important goal of managing an organization.

The manager is a person who occupies a key role in an organization, being responsible for the work of one or more people and having authority over them.[7]

---

4.   C. Possas, *A Especifidade do Quadro Sanitário no Brasil* (Specificity in the Health Picture of Brazil). São Paulo: Hutec, 1989
5.   Selye, cited in Karl Albrecht, *Stress and Manager—Making it work for you.* New York: Simon & Schuster, 1979
6.   Peter Drucker, *A Nova Era da Administracão (The New Era of Administration).* São Paulo: Pioneira de Administração e Negócios, 1970, p.21
7.   W. J. Reddin, Eficácia Gerencial (Managerial Efficacy). São Paulo: Atlas, 1975

Zalesnick,[8] writes that managers tend to see their job as a process of enablement of competencies, involving persons and ideas, interacting to establish strategies and make decisions.

Drucker also emphasizes the responsibility and the role of decision making of the manager: "The manager is the worker gifted with knowledge, who, by virtue of this knowledge, is responsible for the actions and decisions destined to contribute to the productive capacity of his organization."[9]

The manager, according to Caravantes, *"is one who makes decisions and has the function of achieving the objectives of organizations by means of others."*[10] This demands, in a more accentuated way, an adjustment to the organizational environment. Therefore, the manager is subject to continual pressures because production depends on his abilities, and he/she is most vulnerable to stress, since *"to be responsible for people causes more stress than to be responsible for objects."*[11]

Managerial stress affects the manager himself and secondarily causes stress for persons who work as subordinates.

Stress: Historical and Conceptual Aspects

Although the concept of stress is relatively old, the word itself was used during the XVII Century to represent "adversity" or "affliction" and at the end of the Eighteenth Century, its use evolved to mean "force," "pressure" or "effort" exercised primarily by the person himself, his organism, or mind (Rossi).[12] The first author to publish about the concept of stress was Hans Selye.[13]

Other authors have conceptualized stress: "Stress is composed of personal, social, and physiological revolt;"[14] "When internal and external pressures overwhelm the capacity of the person to cope, it provokes an imbalance in the indi-

8. Abraham Zalesnick,"Gerentes e Líderes são Diferentes? (Are Managers and Leaders Different?)" São Paulo: *Nova Cultura*, Vol. 17, 1986

9. Peter Drucker, *O Gerente Eficaz (The Effective Manager)*. Rio de Janeiro: Zahar, 1976, p.17

10. Geraldo R. Caravantes, Administração por Objetivos: uma Abordagem Sócio-Técnica (Management By Objectives: A Socio-Technical Approach). Porto Alegre: FDRH, 1984, p. 19

11. Nelly M. F. Candeias et al., *Stress em Atendentes de Enfermagem (Stress in Health Care Attendants)* Revista Brasileira de Saúde Ocupacional, No. 75, Vol. 20, Jan/Jun 1992, p.22

12. A. M. Rossi, *Autocontrole: Nova Maneira de Controlar o Estresse (Self-Control: New Way to Control Stress)*. São Paulo: Rosa dos Tempos, 1992

13. Hans Selye, *Stress of Life*. New York: McGraw-Hill, 1978

vidual's self-organization. This disorganization we can call stress.[15] For Hans Selye, "stress is a state manifested by a specific syndrome which consists of all the changes not specifically induced within a given biological system."[16]

One can see stress as a necessary part of life, it can be a sign that we are in disequilibria with ourselves and with our environment. This imbalance, if prolonged, creates a state of stress. Stress occurs as part of a process of reaction to changes that occur as much within us (thoughts, feelings, nutrition, manner of breathing) as exterior to us (friends, work, noise, and atmospheric pollution).

When there is a change in our lives we react to it, we alter in some form our physical or psychological balance. The heart rate increases, thoughts and sensations are modified. Eventually we evoke a physiological imbalance that may or may not be temporary. Both positive and negative change can provoke imbalance and stress. For example: an employee that receives unexpectedly a notice of promotion, or contrariwise, a notice of dismissal (two different messages but which cause the same kind of reaction); either message produces a state of imbalance or stress in the same person).

Selye[17] coined the word "stressor" to describe responses to changes which occur in the internal or external world; for example, noise, change in employment, change of boss, divorce, birth of a child. A stressor is an agent that in some way puts pressure on the individual and produces a change or reaction that results in a state of imbalance, even though this may be temporary. Selye labeled this reaction[18] the "stress-reaction." This state of stress results in an accumulation of reactions that occur as a result of different types of stressors.

Cox categorized stress[19] according to its source. He called stress "occupational" when it is a matter of perception by the worker of imbalance between the existing demands of work and his perceived ability to respond to them. The absolute level of demand or expectation is not the most important factor. When there

---

14. Sandra Horn, *Técnicas Modernas de Relaxamento (Modern Techniques of Relaxation)*. São Paulo: Cultrix, 1986, p. 90

15. Arnaldo Loses Filho, et al., *Psiquiatria sem Preconceitos: Um Guia de Psiquitaria para Quem, de Médico e de Louco, Sempre Tem um Pouco (Psychiatry Sans Preconcepts: A Guide to Psychiatry for the Medic or the Loco, Of which Both Are a Little)*. São Paulo: Maltese, 1992, p.101

16. Hans Selye, Op. Cit., p. 12

17. *Ibid.*

18. *Ibid.*

19. Cox, cited by Nell M. F. Candeiras, et al., in *Stress em Atendentes de Enfermagem, Op. Cit.*

is a discrepancy between the perception of demand and the workman's sense of capability to respond adequately, what happens is that stress is often characterized by negative emotions, sensations of unease and general discomfort. Occupational stress can be considered a collection of psychological perturbations or psychic suffering associated with experiences at work.[20]

It is this occupational stress, i.e., the stress strongly associated with working conditions that is the cause not only of unsatisfied employees in the workplace, but also a main cause contributing to their early death. Even if we want to disregard the humanitarian aspects in this issue—an unthinkable absurdity—we cannot forget the multibillion-dollar impact upon society.

Besides, in an organizational society like ours the managers, at every level, have a large responsibility in dealing with people, in obtaining results through them and creating a healthy environment.

In continuing sections we will suggest that old/new technologies, including hypnosis, can have an important role in improving such conditions.

There is much evidence that these equivalents of "self-hypnotic suggestions" can profoundly affect how the body will respond to pain, to heat or cold, to noises, to perceived dangers or threats, including that complex of factors that we have earlier defined as *stress*.

2. MANAGERIAL STRESS AND HYPNOTHERAPY

Next, we want to introduce the technology of hypnosis that can be of value to readers, helping them to increase their degree of self-understanding and to improve their personal performance. Some can question our choice. The reasons are simple: we would like to review information and understanding not only from books, but also from experiences drawn from our personal lives. This is especially true for the topic of hypnosis, which continues to be studied and employed by Caravantes since 1979, when he was moving through the doctoral program at the University of Southern California.[21]

Hypnosis is the technical name given to the observation that "suggestions" in the mind have certain effects on body responses and on actions. Autosuggestion,

---

20.   A. Laville e C. Teiger, *Santé Mentale et Conditions de Travail: Une approache de la psychopathologie du travail,* Revue Therapeutique, 1975; C. Dejours, *A Loucura do trabalho: Estudo de sociopatología do trabalho,* São Paulo: Cortez, 1984; E. Smith and C. O'Brien, "A system for rapid analysis of long-term recordings of heart rate and other physiological parameters," Baltimore: *Biomedical Engineering,* 1986

or self-hypnosis, refers to suggestions we give to ourselves to help us frame or modify responses.

There are many levels of hypnosis and/or self-hypnosis. At the deepest hypnotic levels, the mind tends to limit its attention to stimuli associated with the focus of the "suggestion." That is, in a state we would describe as "hypnotic," the mind has limited its control functions to what it understands to be the intent of the suggestion.

An analogy might be a small group of persons caught up in an emergency, where there are many and competing commands or suggestions as to what best should be done. When a choice or decision is made to listen and respond to only one of the conflicting suggestions, the group becomes focused and concerted action begins. In an analogous way, the mind is normally aware of multiple streams of sensory information competing for conscious attention. When the person chooses to give attention to what seems to be the most important or pressing stream of sensory information, it gives itself the equivalent of a "suggestion" to respond and act in a chosen way.

When awake and alert, the mind is subject to many different stimuli. Somewhere, at some unconscious level, decisions are constantly being made as to what one should do in response to the many stimuli. Some must be disregarded, while others must be attended to. Self-given "suggestions" become guidelines for this unconscious "decider" and affect how the body will respond to the incoming flood of information.

---

21. Caravantes writes: "My first contact with the potentialities of hypnosis date from my youth, when my medical doctor father utilized it in his practice. Further, while living in Santa Monica, while studying in the USC Doctoral program, I decided to invest in a program at the *Institute for Advanced Hypnosis*, in California. In that occasion, besides advancing in the satisfaction of an intellectual need, there was a pressing need: to become physically and mentally capable of passing the Doctoral Qualifying Examinations and researching and writing the doctoral dissertation. The results were so very positive that I continued studies and research into hypnosis. In 1989 and 1990, while I taught in the doctoral program at USC and completed a Post-Doctoral, I studied in the *Esalen Institute*, Big Sur, California, cradle of the Human Potential Movement (Abraham Maslow being the best-known figure). There I continued my research and studies, now combining hypnosis with the emerging neuro-linguistic programming. An organizational clinic, done together with Marina Keiko Nakayama, was enriched by that period of learning. Its objective was performance improvement, especially of executives.

Hypnosis: Origins and Basic Concepts[22]

Traditionally, hypnosis is seen as a social interaction between two people acting in different roles: that of the *hypnotist* and the person hypnotized, or the *subject.* The result of this interaction carries the hypnotized person into a different state of conscious called a *trance.* In this trance state, the behavior of the subject, as well as his experiences, are different from those that characterize habitual behavior when in a state of wakefulness.[23]

There is agreement among practitioners of hypnosis with this definition, although there is a difference of opinion as concerns the specific *nature* of the relationship that is established in hypnosis. There are three approaches to understanding this relationship:

a. *The authoritarian approach*, in which the *powerful individual* (the hypnotist) with reputed special mental abilities, makes the subject (the person hypnotized) move into a passive state in which s/he is predisposed to act on the suggestions of the hypnotist, obeying his/her orders. This is the traditional approach, which could be called *spectacle-hypnosis*, about which there exists an ample folklore, and which has produced, with good reason, an attitude of skepticism and a lack of confidence in its potential, sometimes even to its banishment. The authoritarian approaches to hypnosis arise from its early practitioners and are derived from the writings and practices of historic figures such as Mesmer, Charcot, Bernhein, and Freud. If we focus attention on the power and ability of the hypnotist, the resultant understanding fails to consider the differences among subjects, in terms of their knowledge, beliefs, and personal capacities, as well as their capacity for making choices.

b. *The standard approach.* This is the predominant approach among experimental psychologists. The focus of attention has moved from the hypnotist to the subject, assuming that a greater or lesser susceptibility to hypnosis is derived from some trait or characteristic that is found in the individual. In other words, the subject is, or is not, hypnotizable. The behavior of the hypnotist does not make much difference. Studies produced by E. R. Hillgard,[24]

---

22. The introductory section of this chapter, dealing with hypnosis, draws heavily upon the writings of Stephen G. Gillian, a disciple of renowned therapist, Milton Erickson, who created a revival in the study of hypnosis.
23. Stephen G. Gilligan, *Therapeutic Trances—The Cooperation Principle in Ericksonian Hypnotherapy.* NY: Breunner/Mazel Publishers, 1987

renowned researcher of the University of California, concluded that 15% of subjects are highly susceptible to hypnosis, 65% are moderately susceptible, and 20% are not susceptible. This approach, supported by an extremely positivistic view, has not encouraged others to look into the great variety of techniques being used by different practitioners. The impact of hypnosis has remained short of its therapeutic potential.

c.   *The cooperative approach.* A significant number of newer hypnotherapists start from the principle that in major or minor degree, the susceptibility of the subject to hypnosis stems from complex phenomena which reflect an interaction among motivations and interests of the client, the sensitivity and flexibility of the therapist, and the degree of *rapport* between them.[25] The main proponent of the cooperative approach has been the psychiatrist Milton Erickson, who dedicated sixty years of his life to the research and practice of hypnosis and its uses in psychotherapy. His approach is based entirely upon a framework of cooperation. Erickson writes:

> *...Hypnosis should, first of all, be the result of a situation in which the relationships, inter—and intrapersonal, are developed in a constructive manner to serve both the hypnotist as well as the subject. This cannot be achieved if we continue to follow rigid procedures and fixed methods, neither can they if we press to attain a single and specific objective. The complexity of human behavior and its underlying motivations make necessary an understanding of existing factors in any situation that derives from two personalities engaged in a conjoint activity.*[26]

The cooperative approach emphasizes the existence of a triad:

The hypnotist

The subject

The hypnotist/subject relationships

---

24.   E. R. Hilgard, *Hypnotic Susceptibility.* NY: Harcourt, Brace, Javanovich, 1965

25.   *Rapport:* a term referring to the degree of interaction in the client/therapist, or client/consultant relationship.

26.   Milton Erickson (1952), in E. L. Rossi, ed., "The Collected Papers of M. H. Erickson," in *The Nature of Hypnosis and Suggestion,* Vol. 1., New York: Irvington, 1980

This can be represented in the following diagrammatic form:

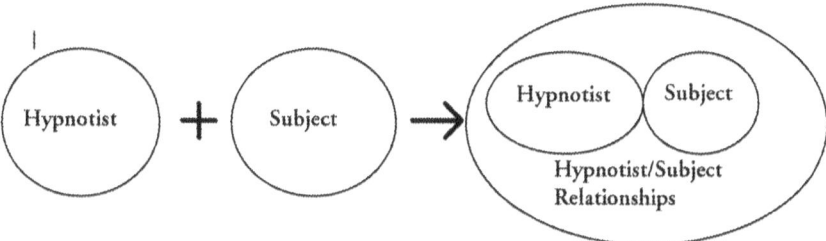

Rossi writes:

> *Whatever the rôle played by the hypnotist, the response from the subject develops in a significant way from active functioning—a functioning that derives from capacities, knowledge, and experiential history of the total personality. The hypnotist can only guide, direct, supervise, and provide opportunities for the subject to realize productive work. To achieve this, the therapist must understand the situation and its necessities, protect the subject completely, and be able to recognize the work being done. He should accept and utilize the emerging behavior and be capable of creating favorable opportunities and situations for the adequate functioning of the subject.*[27]

The approach utilized by Erickson when it employs hypnosis is based on the *principle of utilization*, in which the standards of self-expression of the client, whatever they might be, are understood as contributing to the basis for the development of the therapeutic trance.

Table 8.1 permits a clear visualization of these three approaches, by category:

Table 8.1

Criterion	Authoritarian Approach	Standardized Approach	Cooperative Approach
Situational context	In a theater—On stage	Experimental, in the laboratory	In a therapeutic clinic
Intention	To impress, to fool, to entertain	To study specific phenomena	To create opportunities for transformational changes

27. Milton Erickson (1952), in E. L. Rossi, ed., "The Collected Papers of M. H. Erickson," in *The Nature of Hypnosis and Suggestion*, Vol. 1., New York: Irvington, 1980

Table 8.1 (Continued)

Criterion	Authoritarian Approach	Standardized Approach	Cooperative Approach
Focus	On the hypnotist	On the subject	On a cooperative relationship
Types of communication used by hypnotist	Direct commands	Standardizes suggestions	Extremely flexible, adapted to the needs of the client
Task of the Subject	Expression of bizarre behaviors	Follow experimental suggestions	Develop a personal, intimate experience, in a safe, interpersonal setting
Duration of hypnosis	Brief	Brief	Variable, generally longer (30 to 60 min.)
Interpretation of the non-hypnotic responses	Subject is "resistant"	Subject is not susceptible to hypnosis	The therapist adjusts duration to the needs of the client.
Major Interest	Behavior of the subject	Behavior of the subject	Internal experience of the client and consequent change in behavior

From this point and on, all of our discussion will refer exclusively to the *Ericksonian Approach*, labeled the *Cooperative Approach* in **Table 8.1** above.

Understanding Better the Ericksonian Approach

When we move to understand the way in which Erickson interpreted hypnosis, his conceptualization of it, as well as its useful applications, become clearer. The tone of his approach emphasizes the interpersonal relation between hypnotist and subject, a relationship that is characterized by the principle of *cooperation*. We attempt here to identify other Ericksonian premises:

Each person is unique. Each individual—with his or her values, beliefs, knowledge, motivations, and ways of facing life—constitutes a universe apart, different from that of all other persons. Erickson pointed out that therapeutic communications ought not to be based on theoretical generalizations, nor in statistical probabilities, but rather than in concrete and real norms that represent the self-expression of the individual in the here and now, (including beliefs, behaviors, motivations, symptoms). From this it emerges that the therapist[28] will always initiate his work in a state of *experiential innocence,* that is, treating each situation as a *new situation.* Parting from this premise is the idea that what the client expresses corresponds to an "individualized model of reality." It is a personal universe in the view of that individual.

Hypnosis is an experimental process in the communication of ideas. A good way of understanding hypnosis is to interpret it as a process of communication while walking along, hand in hand, as it were, with the therapist. According to Hartland:

> *...the induction of hypnotic states is above all a process of communication of ideas and an awakening of a flow of thoughts and associations in the client which, in ultimate analysis, will conduct one to behavioral responses...All of these efforts should be realized to give direction to the needs of the client in relation to processes which occur in the client; bodily sensations, memories, emotions, thoughts, feelings, ideas, and past knowledge. A hypnotic technique organized in this way can function admirably well, even in adverse circumstances.*

However, it is important when one interprets hypnosis as a process of communication to keep in mind that its objective is *experiential participation* and not conceptual understanding. (Parenthetically, we encounter this problem as we write these words, since we attempt to conceptualize and explain hypnosis so that you can understand it, when what we really should be doing is to seek a way in which you can live the experience, in the here and now.)

Each person depends upon his/her own internal resources. All of us have at our disposal internal resources permitting us to live a life minimally satisfactory (we would risk to say, even *happy*). However, this potential seems to be disassociated with the way in which people live day to day. They work based upon certain ideas and premises without ever questioning their source or validity. For example, each of us, theoretically, is able to be courteous to people that we know, whether in the family or at work. However, few people adopt such an attitude for daily living: they pass their entire life as though they lived on a battlefield. Others manage to be courteous to only a few people (wife, children). The work of Erickson is concentrated upon awakening our attention to the fact that people do not need

---

28. We will use the terms hypnotist and therapist as interchangeable, understanding hypnosis as a medium to be employed by someone (therapist or hypnotherapist) in the search for improved communication with the other party (subject, or client).

to let small things pile up. The function of the therapist is to awaken in people the capability of utilizing that which they have at their disposal, but which needs to be focused in a different way.

The hypnotic trance permits the strengthening of internal resources. One of the more important benefits of the hypnotic trance is that it permits, during its duration, that *models* adopted by the individual undergo modifications and alterations, permitting the restructuring and reorganization of the person's ways of conceptualizing phenomena. The premise is that conscious activity, oriented by objectives, typically involves the utilization of a mental model that narrows the focus of our attention on stimuli that are considered *relevant. Relevant*, in this case, must be clearly understood. It means to be *in agreement* with the parameters fixed by the model in use.

Many times the model is in absolute disagreement with the lived situation of the individual. However, he cannot manage to conceive of a world outside of this model. This conceptual trap becomes cyclical, repetitive, an endless *loop* of reprising errors, reaffirming solutions that no longer function. The hypnotic trance is able to create conditions in which the individual comes to have access to internal resources available in abundance so that transformational change can become operative, creating a personal state of high receptivity in which new ways of being can be developed.

The emphasis is on the correction of course rather than on past errors. The Ericksonian approach concentrates its attention on the achievement of objectives and present needs and not on an understanding of the past. His approach is extremely positive: the past signifies multiple learnings, often forgotten or not valued adequately; the present offers an infinite number of opportunities for new knowledge and self-appreciation; the future is an open field for self-development. Therefore, that which the client possesses—his knowledge, models, understandings, independently of qualifying adjectives such as *good or bad*—comes to be utilized as the basis for a walk into new learning.

The therapist, following this approach, orients the client toward the clarification of his objectives and interests; the client, on creating opportunities so that he can achieve them. This orientation emphasizes *self-development* as a natural, biological course of personal evolution of the individual, and problems or errors as deviations or detours from that plan. This vision was very well explored by Pearce:

> *A biological scheme of magnificent proportions…is constructed by our genes. The scheme is flexible so as to accommodate an infinite number of variables. Develop-*

ment means to learn to move in agreement with this system built into us. As is natural, with every advance, initial movement is precarious. We stumble, trip, fall. The fact that we trip and fall is incidental because eventually we become capable of maintaining our eyes on that orienting line of development—as long as we maintain ourselves aligned. Everything develops in its appropriate time when we act in this way, and the stumbling and major diversions have little long-term significance.[29]

The idea that every person is unique can be interpreted on several levels.
Stephen Gillian, disciple of Milton Erickson, utilizes an approach very similar to that of Roberto Assagioli to study the different levels. He establishes four different levels: **a) the deep self; b) the unconscious mind; c) the conscious mind; and d) the contents of consciousness.** Each of these levels can be viewed as a concentric circle (see the following **Figure 8.2**).

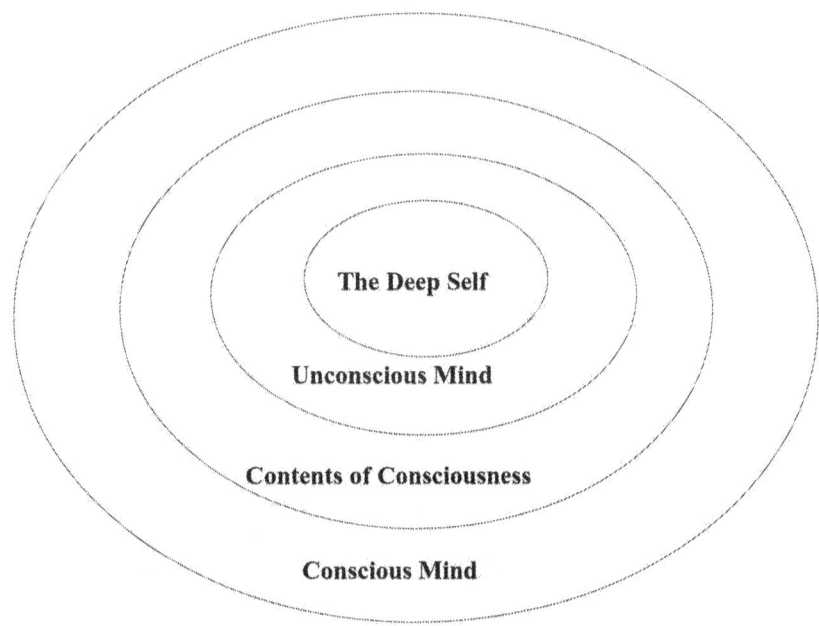

Figure 8.2 Individual Levels

---

29.   J. C. Pearce, *The Bond of Power.* New York: E. P. Dutton, 1981, p. 92

a) The Deep Self constitutes the very essence of the Self, that in Erickson's words, is the *vital sense of the self* and which many times is not taken into consideration. This essence cannot be captured by any image, description or other form. It is its rhythm and identity that characterizes a person as a unique being. Gilligan writes:

> [The Deep Self]…is the essence of the vital energy and of generational capacity. It is indivisible, being a whole naturally integrated. I see that one of the tasks of generative hypnotherapy is to reconnect the client with his Deep Self by means of explorations based in hypnosis.[30]

b) The unconscious mind: a differentiation of the *self* over time gives origin to an organizational identity system conventionally called the *unconscious mind.* The *mind* is a tool, a computational instrument, of surprising informational capacity, whose function is to preserve the integrity of the *self*, augmenting, at the same time, its autonomy.

According to Bateson[31], the mind is a cybernetic system constructed of closed (circular) information *loops* or networks by means of which distinctions are noted and ideas identified and transmitted. Thus, the mind holds a map of the territory, expressing and representing the correlation of the self to its context. It is a structure (pattern) and a structuring of relations, a matrix or constellation by which we distinguish and navigate the "space" that surrounds us.

Interpreting the mind in this way, it cannot be understood as being contained within the physical body. We believe that Bateson tells this in an admirable way:

> …the delimitation of the individual mind depends always upon the phenomena that we desire to understand or explain. Obviously, there exists a great number of ways to acquire information external to our skin, and they, as well as messages that are transported, need to be included as part of the relevant mental system.[32]
> The individual mind is immanent, but not only in the body; it is immanent in vias of information and in messages from outside of our body; and there is a greater mind, of which the individual mind is a subsystem. This greater mind is perhaps what we want to call God…immanent in the social system and totally interconnected with planetary ecology.[33]

---

30. Stephen Gilligan, *Therapeutic Trances.* New York: Breunner/Mazel, 1987. p.21
31. G. Bateson, *Steps to an Ecology of Mind.* New York: Ballantine, 1972. p. 461
32. Idem., p. 458
33. Idem., p. 461

This idea of integral man is found in the work of Alan Watts. His is a concept of a non-encapsulated, non-limited man, who does not admit as his external frontier the skin that covers his flesh and bones. He understands as false the image that persons usually fashion of themselves—an ego inside of its enclosing skin. This is made sufficiently clear when Alan Watts affirms that:

> *What we really are, in first place, is the entirety of our body. Although our body is covered with a skin—I am capable of differentiating my external from my internal parts—my body cannot exist except in a determined type of natural environment. Obviously it requires air, and this air should be of a determined temperature; it requires nutrition, needs to be on a certain type of planet, close to a certain type of star that rotates regularly and in a manner rhythmic and harmonic, in order than life can be maintained. This arrangement is essential to the existence of my body, as well as all of my internal organs—my heart, my brain, my lungs, and so forth. In this way, there is no way to separate me, as a physical being, from the natural environment in which I live.*[34]

c) ***The conscious mind:*** this may be seen as a *figure* in relation to the *field,* or the field of the unconscious. While the unconscious mind tends to act holistically, the conscious mind is linear in orientation. Its primordial function consists in structuring information in *models* or *programs* of action and in establishing and calculating conceptual relationships. The conscious mind can be interpreted as a manager or regulator, whose function is conservation and not the generation of new alternatives. Its area is the management of roles, of plans for achieving objectives, of scripts, strategies, structures and rationality.

d) ***The contents of consciousness,*** which consists of those elements that filter up from the mind and which include individual perceptions, motor activities, images, cognitions and sensations.

Integrating the elements just analyzed (a, b, c, & d), we can summarize as follows:

> *A person can be understood as being a unique essence (self) operating within a unique psychological organizational system (unconscious mind of the self), using strategies unique and peculiar to achieve objectives (conscious mind or the self structure) and being absorbed, during a determined period of time, with distinctive mental contents (contents of the self).*[35]

---

34. Alan Watts, *The Essential Alan Watts.* California: Celestial Arts, 1977. p. 34
35. Op. cit., p. 24

The Role of Hypnosis in Relation to the Conscious/ Unconscious

Various thinkers have proposed the conscious/unconscious distinction over the years. The approach of Erickson starts from the principle that the two systems are complementary in nature, however, he considers the conscious mind as responding to the unconscious system.

The conscious mind is clever, alert, and efficient. However, the unconscious mind is necessary for knowledge and renovation. When the two are in conflict, or are not synchronized, there is little doubt that the unconscious mind establishes the parameters and dominates the process.

Complementarities in Conscious/Unconscious Characteristics

Suggested By	Unconscious	Conscious
C. S. Smith	Global	Atomistic
Price	Synthetic or Concrete	Analytic or Reductionistic
Wilder	Geometric	Numeric
Head	Percentual or Non-Verbal	Symbolic or Systematic
Goldstein	Concrete	Abstract
Reusch	Analogic or Eidetic	Digital or Discursive
Bateson	Analogical	Digital
J. Z. Young	Similar to a Map	Abstract
Hobbes	Free and Disordered	Directed
Freud	Primary Processes	Secondary Processes
Bruner	Metaphorical	Rational
Radhakrishnan	Integral	Rational

(Adapted from Bogen, 1969)

We can affirm that the unconscious processes are intelligent, organized, and holistic, permitting high creativity. Furthermore, they operate autonomously from conscious processes and are capable of deep transformational changes.

Thus, instead of considering the hypnotic process as one in which suggestions are "planted" in a passive receptacle, the Ericksonian approach conceptualizes the trance as a process in which conscious aspects of the client are put to one side, or in an open space, permitting significant transformations to occur. It is important to recognize that **conscious *insight* is not necessary for changes to happen**. In other words, by means of a well-conducted hypnotic process it is possible effectively to change behavior without consciously understanding *how* or *why* it happened.

We can say that all too often people hold a limited vision of the potentialities of their combined conscious/unconscious because they see themselves in a restricted way, emphasizing only the processes belonging to the conscious mind, thereby disassociating themselves from a source much richer and more promising represented by their unconscious (See Figure 8.3).

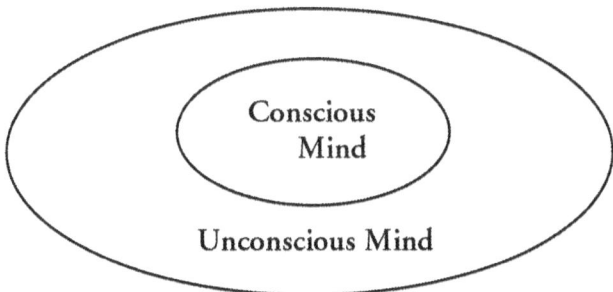

Figure 8.3 Conscious and Unconscious Mind

The role of the hypnotist is to establish an integration between the conscious and unconscious, in a programmed and systematic way, reeducating the individual, opening up the benefits derived from a combined use of the conscious/ unconscious faculties.

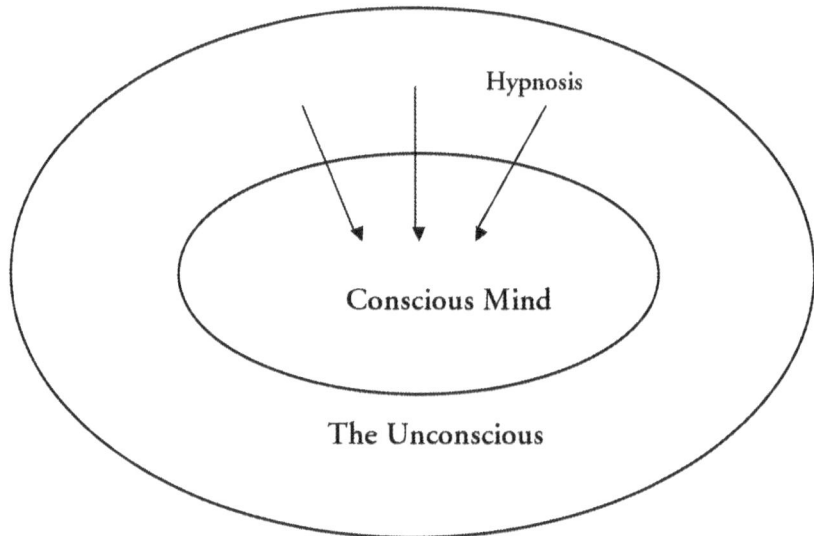

Figure 8.4 Hypnosis: Opening a channel of communication

Hypnosis and Self-Hypnosis

Until now we have emphasized the presence of three elements in the process of hypnosis—the hypnotist, the subject being hypnotized, and the relationship between hypnotist and subject. Actually we have done this because usually hypnosis is understood in a therapeutic context, where it is used as an instrument by the therapist to obtain a greater degree of interaction with the client in order to proceed with the necessary and desired therapeutic modifications. However, the hypnotist's role is dispensable, that of a facilitator, auxiliary only to the process of hypnosis, since *all hypnosis is essentially self-hypnosis.* This fact is of extreme importance, because after a training period, anyone—and this includes executives—can, without the assistance of another person, make use of self-hypnosis and obtain all of the positive results potentially flowing from this new state of consciousness.

For purposes of comparison, self-hypnosis, respecting its particularities, can be considered to be very similar to *deep meditation,* where the person has generated a nearly total abstraction from the external environment, with a nearly total concentration on an internal focus point chosen by the individual.

Hypnosis: Stress Reduction and Time Distortion

The success of the enterprise is a direct consequence of the health and skills of its managerial group. The managerial team analyzes objectives, formulates strategies, decides on principal directions, allocates resources, and invests a major part of its life, time and potential to the construction of a viable organization.

One way for executives to collaborate in the maintenance of positive stress for the managerial team is to improve the abilities of the management team by means of *training*. An investment in improved health and quality of work for managers is fundamental to the well being of the organization.

Training Program for the Reduction of Stress and Curing Associated Illnesses.

Carl Simonton, ex-director of the Cancer Council and Research Center of Dallas, Texas, oncologist, specialist, with his wife, Stephanie, psychologist and director of counseling, have developed an approach for the control of stress and a search for the healing of illnesses such as cancer. Their approach is based on two elements that can, with relative ease, be obtained by means of the quasi-hypnotic techniques: *relaxation and visualization.*[36]

The usefulness of *relaxation* by itself, in a world of tense people, is already conceded. For those who experienced total relaxation via hypnosis it will not be too difficult to accept our affirmation that "if relaxation were the only product of hypnosis, the investment made is already worth the effort."

Visualization, along with being an extremely efficient instrument of motivation for the recuperation of health, as we will see, goes very well together with relaxation. It can contribute to the improvement of development in all areas of one's life, including such as sports, studies, and sex.

Because of the simplicity of the suggested scenarios, we will transcribe literally a sequence proposed by the Simontons. The starting point is a kind of relaxation exercise, with its concomitant reduction of stress.

---

36. Carl Simonton, Stephanie M. Simonton and James L. Creighton, *Com a Vida de Novo, (With a New Life)* São Paulo: Summus Editorial, 1978

Relaxation/Visualization for healing.

Many readers may desire to use mental images to help free themselves of pain and illnesses. The Simontons present a brief mental exercise that can be utilized to enable a person's mind and body to work together in the healing of various kinds of illnesses. The exercise employs standard techniques of stress reduction induced by means of visualizing scenarios that are associated with relaxation, lowered stress, and ultimately, healing.

1. Create a mental image of the illness or pain that you actually have, visualizing it in a manner that has meaning for you.

2. Imagine the treatment that you are receiving and see it eliminating the source of the illness or pain, or perhaps, of strengthening the capacity of your body to heal itself.

3. Imagine the natural defenses of your body, and its natural processes helping in eliminating the causes of the illness or pain.

4. Imagine yourself healthy and free of the illness or pain.

5. See yourself achieving, in a successful manner, the objectives that you have established for yourself.

6. Give yourself praise for participating in your healing. See yourself doing this exercise of relaxation/visualization several (three) times daily, emerging awake and alert each time you do so.

7. Prepare yourself to open your eyes and to become conscious of the space where you are.

8. Open your eyes and prepare to take up your normal activities.

Holistic vs. Alternative approaches

The approach of Simonton is *not* called an *alternative* approach, because it does not abandon conventional medical treatments. Simonton is a physician, trained according to the parameters of traditional treatment of diseases. However, he does encourage patients to think holistically (whole=total, entire). Western culture is educated in a kind of reasoning called dualistic, introduced to Western culture by the early Greek philosopher, Aristotle. Aristotelian, or formal, logic is based upon a principle of exclusion: its logic operates by forcing a decision that case 'A' either belongs, or does not belong, to the class 'A'. This kind of thinking tends to displace a holistic logic, which is *integrative*.[37] Holistic thinking takes into account *both/and* options rather than limiting itself to *either/or* choices. The terms *conventional* or *alternative* are merely adjectives that refer to a same reality, one and indivisible: the human being.

Some illustrative uses of self-hypnosis

A few brief examples will be useful to illustrate the use of hypnosis for its potential beneficial impact in different life arenas. In paragraphs above, we mentioned physical and mental health, and enhanced learning and creativity. In the section that follows, we turn to an application of self-hypnosis to time-management, given its universal importance to managers.

Time Administration, or How to Distort Time Usefully

Effectiveness is a habit, a complex of practical norms that we incorporate into repeated activities. There are essentially five of these practices, according to Peter Drucker, that should be acquired in order to become an effective manager. The first is that effective managers are more focused on results than on the work in itself. Secondly, effective managers build on their own strengths and on those of their superiors in the organization. They always begin with what they are intending to do, and do not focus on the difficulties and barriers, at times seemingly immovable. Third, they try to establish priorities, concentrating their forces on those areas where results can be obtained. Fourth, effective managers make effective decisions, adopting studied strategies and not merely improvised tactics. Last, and most importantly, effective managers know how to use their time efficiently. Without this skill, the others are difficult or impossible.

It seems valid to weave some considerations about the factor of time and how different persons deal with time before attempting to place it rationally in organizational terms. The truth is that from region to region, from culture to culture, we have different ideas about time. In other words, each culture has its own characteristic and appropriate rhythm.

> *F. M. Esfandiary, an Iranian romanticist and essayist, tells a story about a collision between two different cultural rhythms when German engineers, during the period prior to the Second World War, found themselves helping in the construction of a railroad in Iran. The Iranians, along with inhabitants of the Middle*

---

37. See Geraldo Caravantes and Wesley Bjur, *ReAdministração em Ação. São Paulo: Makron Books, 1996,* pp. 46-51, where the authors develop the concept of an integrative logic, supported by an eclectic paradigm, one the authors call "fuzzy logic."

East in general, assume a fairly relaxed attitude in relation to time, more so than North Americans or Western Europeans. When work gangs of Iranians continually arrived ten minutes or so late for work assignments, the Germans, themselves super-punctual and always working under pressure, tended to terminate the employment of these "wise men of the East." The Iranian engineers had their difficulties in attempting to convince their German counterparts that, according to standards of the Middle East, the workmen were being heroically punctual, and that if the terminations continued, soon there would be no able workmen available to continue the job, other than women and children.[38]

There is little doubt that people live with different ideas concerning their conceptualization of time. An extremely common complaint from North American executives when working outside of their country can be translated into two types of questions:

Why do foreign counterparts arrive so late to business meetings? When Americans and foreigners meet, why do the foreign nationals take so long to arrive at the issue under discussion?

We need not go very far in search of examples. Within Brazil, we observe different rhythms of life and time schedules peculiar to different regions: the Paulist (São Paulo) time, in which there almost identity between the formal and real times; the Carioca (Rio de Janeiro) time, in which an hour of tardiness is not even considered "tardy."

Individual conditionings are as much or more important than the cultural. For diverse reasons, characteristics such as age differences make persons perceive time in different ways. Persons of advanced years are those who have a greater probability to react strongly against any exterior alteration imposed as a social transformation. There is a solid computational base for an observation frequently associated with conservatism: time passes more rapidly for the elderly.

When a father of fifty years of age says to his son of fifteen that he will have to wait two years in order to have his own automobile, this interval of 730 days represents about four percent of the father's lifetime at that moment. But it represents more than thirteen percent of the life duration of the youth. Therefore, it is not strange to understand that for the youth, the wait will seem to be three or four times longer than it would seem to the father. Identically, two hours in the life of a child of four years can be felt as the equivalent of twelve hours in the life of his 24 year-old mother. Asking the small child to wait for two hours to receive a sweet is equivalent to asking the mother to wait fourteen hours for her cup of coffee.

---

38. Reported in Alvin Toffler, *O Choque do Futuro (Future Shock)*. Rio de Janeiro: Artenova, 1973, p.31

There can also be a biological base for similar differences in subjective responses to the passage of time. With advancing age, psychologist John Cohen, of the University of Manchester, indicates that calendar years seem to get progressively shorter. In retrospect, each year seems shorter than the one that has just ended. Possibly as a consequence of the attenuation of biological rhythms, the world seems to be moving more rapidly for elderly persons, whether or not that is true.[39]

Time presents diverse characteristics, which we can proceed to conceptualize:

Inelasticity: The supply of time is absolutely inelastic, that is, the day has only 24 hours and not a minute more. Whatever be the quantity of demand, the supply will not grow.

Perishability: Being entirely perishable, time cannot be stored or stockpiled. Yesterday's time is forever lost and will never return. For this reason, there is always a deficient supply of available time.

Insubstitutability: Within certain limits we can often substitute one element for another, copper for aluminum, or capital for human labor. We can use more knowledge and more effort. However, there is no substitute for time. Everything requires time. It is the only condition that is truly universal. Whatever work is realized uses time.

Although a majority of executives are forever preoccupied with planning their use of time, often they complain that their well-intentioned plans remain limited to the paper on which they were written.

The reason, although simple, is not usually recognized. We know that in any type of production, the limiting factor is the one that is least abundant. This element, in function of characteristics pointed out earlier, is the factor of time. Thus, however meritorious the intention, even the most sophisticated planning achieves nothing if one lacks the time necessary for its implementation.

This is not the place to develop a methodology for the diagnosis of executive use and eventual rationalization of time, but we want to point out that we cannot do without such a rationalization. We recognize the near obsession of some authors in relation to the administration of time. The word *rational* is the nucleus of what we want to leave with the reader. Understanding *rational* as one of the best uses of consciousness, where rationality is found there is a chance to function well in an organizational society.

While we were developing a methodology for the rational use of time, we were aware that something was lacking. In the search for potential applications of hypnosis we came to perceive the possibilities that it offers for a better management

---

39. Toffler, *op.cit.,* p.30

of time. Then we came upon the concept of *time distortion* under hypnosis—a technique that permits the mind to work out complex designs, develop plans, hypotheses and scenarios, all in a matter of a few minutes.

In hypnosis, the subject can perceive a few minutes as though they were hours or an entire day. The psychiatrist I. F. Cooper, of Phoenix, Arizona relates that an executive under this orientation achieved a quantity of new ideas during a few seconds when earlier it had taken more than three hours to register on paper his inspirations and insights.[40]

In one of the first experiences of temporal distortion recounted by Dr. Milton Erickson, a secondary school student interested in fashion design imagined herself seated at a table looking at a department store display window, thinking and then designing for the models she was visualizing. She imagined that approximately an hour had passed. In truth, hardly ten seconds by the watch had passed. The new style was already sketched in her mind. Normally she would have spent several hours per session until the new design was sketched.

Gay Gaer Luce, a writer of scientific issues, has suggested that perhaps there are "natural" units of biological time for the central nervous system that are available for to the individual. They can be considered a potential that we may or may not utilize.

> *...Only future research will be able to tell us if these biological units of time are similar to the units administered by our clocks. Studies on the hypnotic distortion of time emphasis how limited our cultural vision is of the sense of time, and how we will be able to help in the enrichment of the education of youth by means of more and better learning in early years of schooling. A significant number of scientists judge that any ten year old with a reasonable degree of intelligence could possess the knowledge of a secondary school student. Children, using techniques of the distortion of time, can accelerate their personal processes of learning.*[41]

One of the authors (Caravantes) used the technique of temporal distortion to accelerate the process of the elaboration of his Doctoral Dissertation, a normally lengthy process involving the choice of a topic, research of a supporting bibliography, the organization of ideas, and the act itself of writing several hundred pages. Given these conditions, those few who manage to complete their exams and move on to write a dissertation usually take a year or more to complete the pro-

---

40.   Reported in Marilyn Ferguson, *The Brain Revolution.* New York: Bantam Books, 1975

41.   Gay Gaer Luce in Marilyn Ferguson, *op. cit.*

cess. In the specific case of which we speak, the effective time given to this task was reduced to six months, with the delivery of the completed dissertation of sufficient merit to be later transformed into a published book.

Our conclusion is that the hypnotic distortion of the sense of time is less centered on technique, and more focused on a way of conceptualizing the world. It sees time not in terms of 24 hours by the clock, of present, past, or future, although such segmentations can help us in social and organizational lives. Temporal distortion sends us into notion of global and indivisible time, in which we are immersed and drenched. Such a concept takes us to another level of perception and reflection, where we are viewed as global beings, outside of, and beyond the many limitations established by contemporary paradigms that demonstrate a decreasing explanatory power. Such paradigms are not only less useful, but worse, they condition us to be less effective than we can be.

Chapter 9:
Managing the Conscious/
Unconscious Interface

"According to an Arab legend, a blind man wandering, lost in a forest, tripped and fell. Feeling around, he discovered that he had fallen next to a crippled man. The two began to converse, each lamenting his bad luck. The blind man complained, "I don't know how long I have wandered, lost in this forest, unable to find my way out." To which the crippled man responded, "And I don't know how long I have laid here, unable to get up and leave." They continued to converse, until at some point the lame man exclaimed: "Now I know!—You will carry me on your back and I will point you the way. Together we will find our way out of the forest." According to the fable, the blind man symbolizes rationality, and the lame man symbolizes intuition. We can only find our way out of the forest when we learn to integrate both of these capabilities."

—Peter Senge

"The response to challenges comes from pure, creative thought. When this response ceases, the society begins its inexorable decline."

—Toynbee

What You Will Find In This Chapter—

—The hyperstability of rationalized organizations

—Integration of Reason/Intuition: A Source of Creativity

—Carl Rogers and the Search for a Theory of Creativity

Human Society at a Threshold of Change

The history of humanity, if analyzed retrospectively, is a parade of changes of greater or lesser magnitude. However, the changes can be considered the theme of a larger historic process. The Twentieth Century, and most especially its last quarter, acquired a surprising rhythm of change.

Organizations and social institutions, previously somewhat responsive to the needs of people and the problems they face, have become slowly weakened, less agile, bowed under the weight of new problems and challenges for which they were never prepared. Actually, an organizational inventory or audit, whether in the European, American, or the Brazilian contexts, will reveal a collection of organizations, which fall short of the present needs of their clients. Existing organizations tend to respond in reactionary ways. Apparently, they are incapable of anticipating and proposing alternatives to the problems now appearing.

Many executives, whether in the public or private sectors, do not perceive that the human adventure is at a threshold of history. As is inevitable in every period of transition, a certain number of institutions will disappear, others will be transformed, and a few will grow and develop. Two things are certain: a) all will be affected in some form or another by the new global conditions, and b) to live through great changes requires flexibility and wisdom.

Restructuring bureaucracies for the non-stability

Historically, public and private organizations are designed for stability. Bureaucratic organizations, which focus on routine and efficiency in predictable environments, well exemplify this affirmation. It seems that now the time has come in which we will have to re-structure ourselves no longer for stability, but rather for change. The critical question will come to be: How shall we put into march, cultivate, and cause to flourish a process whose characteristic is marked by change and no longer stability? The institutionalization of a process of change should be the concern of our society and organizations. Isolated efforts, or stagnated and partial searches for organizational improvement are no longer sufficient to the need.

John Gardner,[1] commenting on the nature of self-renewing individuals and organizations, affirms that what characterizes both is their capacity for experi-

---

1.   John Gardner, *Self-Renewal: The Individual and the Innovative Society*. New York: Perennial Library, 1963.

mentation, to be less concerned with precedent, with convention, with rules and written regulations. A disposition to take risks, to overcome challenges in order to experience continual learning, seem to be the critical characteristics of societies and organizations that maintain themselves in vital and continual self-renewal. The organizational and institutional apparati predominant in today's society reflect the perceptions of a distorted environment, of limited cognitive capacities, and of elitist political processes that are myopic, unmindful of the needs of the larger environment.

The critical problems which humanity faces, including the worsening pollution of air and water, the exhaustion of non-renewable natural resources, or the threat of nuclear war, are the creation, product and consequence of man himself. In order that humans and their institutions can survive, many transformations and much learning must occur.

The great challenge, which we face, is the search for a self-renewing society, that is, one immune to decadence and entropy. John Gardner sees such a society as a society of free men, where individual liberty is achieved through self-understanding and where formal education is only part of this global process of learning.

> *"For the self-renewing man, the development of his potentialities and processes of self-discovery never end. Because of this, he is highly motivated, creative, and innovative, respecting the sources of his own energy and motivation."*[2]

And this man capable of self-renewal, with all certainty cannot be the product of training, pure and simple.

Paulo Freire: From Training to Development

Paulo Freire is a Brazilian author of several highly regarded books on the role of education as an agent of change. He emphasizes the importance of the right kind of education, an education that leads to self-reflexive learning and autonomy of the individual. Freire affirms that a capacity for self-reflection and a continuing search for the meaning of human existence is at the root of all learning.

1) The capacity for self-reflection moves one to the development of what Freire calls a "critical conscience." This, in its turn, permits the reorganization of personal experience, transforming their picture of reality. In this manner, even though the person maintains his/her identity from birth until death, there is a

---

2.   John Gardner, *op. cit.*

continual process of modification that is the product of day-to-day learning. One's identity is maintained while at the same time it is being self-renewed.

2) On the other hand, a fundamental nucleus of learning resides in the fact that man is, and recognizes he is, an "unfinished being," involved in a permanent search for perfection, that he can be the subject, and never the object, of learning.

Man is educated with a notion of time. Man is an historic being, living in the present, but with a dimension of the past and with a capacity, based upon past experiences, to construct a future. Education has, therefore, an historic dimension that is only found in human society. "Animals do not have a sense of time. They only have the present. Because of this, animals can only be trained, domesticated, conditioned, but never educated."[3]

Learning looks toward the liberation of humans, to the growth, and in a majority of cases, to the conquest of individual autonomy. Learning permits mankind the use of free will, the capacity to choose among alternatives, to select options with a clear understanding of their consequences, and to be creative and innovative. We know that creativity and innovation are only developed in a context of freedom. However, learning occurs effectively only at the moment in which the incorporation of learning is translated into a creative *praxis*.

Another thing Freire affirms is that learning does not come in a unidirectional manner, flowing from maestro to disciple, but rather through participation, through giving and receiving in a dialogue that nourishes both master and learner in the construction of a view of reality which emerges. He sees reality not as a given: we construct it by means of our personal participation in the decisions of the present as we mold the future. In this sense, we affirm that the future is today and depends upon us. If we learn to stimulate the autonomy of our fellow man, it will necessarily reinforce critical thought, the basis of freedom and liberty of expression. As a consequence, learning is linked to the definition of humankind itself, that which differentiates us from other living species, linked to our rationality.

Caravantes[4] has marked a clearer distinction between the "trained" and the "developed" individuals. The "trained" person is specifically prepared to carry on a given task or a predetermined function, and not to offer any criticisms of its validity. He is capable of implementing with more or less precision whatever he was ordered to do. Nothing more.

---

3.   Paulo Freire, *Educação e Mudança*. Rio de Janeiro: Paz e Terra, 1979
4.   G. R. Caravantes, "Tecnology apropriada para o desenvolvimento de Recursos Humanos—Uma nova abordagem." In G. Caiden and G. Caravantes, *Reconsideração do Conceito de Desenvolvimento*. Caxias do Sul, Ed. UCS, 1988

What Is Meant By "Developed" Human Resources?

1) "Developed" individuals are conscious that reality is not over there someplace, external to themselves, waiting to be discovered. Rather, each of us is an effective participant in the creation of the social reality in which we live, even though the character of this participation can be different from one individual to another. It is important for each person to position himself as a thinker, self-actualizing, active in relation to himself and the world. If, on the contrary, he is merely reactive, he loses the substance of being real, turning himself into a mere system of information processing, passive in relation to the society that models his life; incapable of transcending it.

This means abandoning a defensive attitude in favor of an attitude in which the individual becomes progressively more capable to listen to himself, to experience what is happening inside as well as what is happening outside of the self.

2) As a consequence, the developed individual, educated in the manner we propose, gives himself to the exercise of a critical reflection, perception, and analysis of the context in which he lives. He goes beyond the frontiers of his limited organizational world. Carl Rogers tells us that these are individuals who are increasingly open to growth and experience.

This reflexive man, active in relation to himself and the world, open to experience, is necessarily tolerant, flexible, and adaptable. In accepting the complexity in himself that the human condition imposes, he will necessarily accept it in others.

You will not see a rigid narrow view in this man, nor the imposition of a pre-elaborated structure for responding to new experience. The unformed, amorphous, individual of industrial society applies a prefabricated structure to his perception of reality, deforming it so that it will fit into his preconceived ideas, and not even ideas that are his, but those inherited from his culture. The "developed" man is one who is interjected with notions of experimentation, of less concern with precedent, with conventional rules and regulations. He is one who forges ahead, who projects himself as an autonomous human being, and who is prepared to accept the responsibility of re-inventing his humanity.

How Shall We Develop This Human?

How does one set in motion, cultivate, cause to flourish, a process whose tone is one of change and not stability? How can persons become conscious of the riches that are contained in ideas of uncertainty, of being unfinished, of incompletion?

Why are questions always more important than answers? How shall we adapt the spirit of an individual to what is happening just now? How shall we guarantee creative individuals, capable of giving innovative responses to the growingly complex problems that our organizational society is facing at the beginning of a new millennium?

The Integration of Reason-Intuition: The Source of Creativity

We understand creativity to be the response of the individual to questions about his survival as a species. A turbulent and changing world demands responses different from the usual, since what used to work no longer functions. However, we achieve nothing by merely saying: *"Be creative!"* because this probably will not alter behaviors. Perhaps we might end up even more confused.

In the work of Carl Rogers,[5] with his lengthy experience as a therapist during a long and fruitful life, we search for some ideas to better explain not only the concept of creativity, but also how we should go about searching for it. We will attempt to be faithful to Roger's line of thinking in what follows:

The substrate of all human motivation is an organic tendency, innate in the individual, to search for self-actualization. This tendency begins with the simple satisfaction of the basic necessities, of hunger, thirst, sex, safety, and even the higher one of self-realization. In summary, to wrestle with life as humans, we are always, by definition, wrestling with a tendency to be active, to be searching for something.

There exists something like a central source of energy in the human organism, which can be highly trusted. It functions for the entire organism, not only for a part, and can be interpreted as a dynamic tendency in search of satisfaction and not merely a function of maintenance.

When we analyze human behavior, however, sometimes we encounter a true puzzle: *many persons seem to be at war with themselves.* While their organisms are vitally constructed for self-fulfillment, their consciousness seems to reveal an opposing tendency, generating conflict between conscious and unconscious directives. The consequence is self-defeating behavior, such as a neurosis; an inability to face life, as in a psychosis; unhappiness and internal division as in the maladjustments that occur in all of us. Why does this occur? How shall we

---

5.   Carl Rogers, *Tornar-se Pessoa (On Becoming a Person)*. São Paulo: Martins Fonte, 1977

explain that a person can be consciously fighting for one objective, while their entire organism seems to follow another orientation?

Rogers uses the metaphor of a pyramid to answer these questions. In his search for an answer he felt it necessary to reflect on the nature of conscious awareness in the life of the individual. According to Rogers, the ability to focus attention seems to be one of the last to evolve in the human species. He treats it as the smallest piece, the apex only, of a vast pyramid, which represents the relationships between the conscious and non-conscious parts of the mind. (See Figure 9.1)

Another analogy to represent the relationship between conscious/unconscious is to imagine the functioning of the individual as an enormous pyramidal fountain shaped. The apex is intermittently illuminated by the light of conscious awareness. The normal flow of life in a person who is functioning well does not require this quality of special awareness to be activated often. Rather, the unconscious "takes care of things" for us, calling on conscious awareness only when triggered by something out of the ordinary. This *"unconscious-consciousness"* tends to be a kind of reflection of normality rather than a focus of special attention. Perhaps it might be more accurate to say that in such a person, consciousness is the *reflection of something, of the flow of the organism at that moment;* something normal, which does not demand attention.

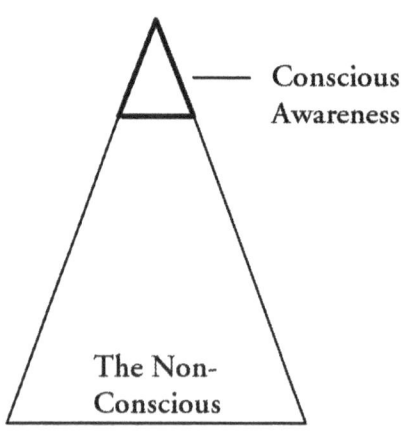

Figure 9.1

Only when "normal" functioning is disturbed does this self-conscious awareness surge up. It is as if a light turns on, calling attention to something, which for some reason, merits special attention.

Lancelot Whyte, philosopher and historian of science, arrives at a similar conclusion as Rogers, but following a different line of thought. He says that in a person who is functioning normally, free and spontaneous activity, including the transitory rhythms of eating, drinking, walking, loving, doing things, working, thinking, dreaming, do not evoke a persistent, differentiated consciousness. When we feel that good or normal things are going on we can forget them, as a general rule. When functioning in this way, with the non-conscious taking care of the normal and good, the person can be considered integrated and unitary.[6]

Rational Intuition and Intuitive Rationality:

In relation to Rogers and Whyte, both authors reinforce the idea of the large disproportion between conscious awareness and the non-conscious parts of the mind, between the rational and the intuitive parts of our cognitive capabilities. The non-conscious seems to occupy most of the pyramid base, the conscious awareness only a modest apex. Also note that the view these authors present of the non-conscious is very close to that of Milton Erickson. It is a very positive and rich view of the unconscious (i.e., intuitive) as an informational base that contains all that we need to know in order better to live our lives. Erickson, treating this conscious/unconscious relationship would say: "Your conscious mind is very intelligent, but your unconscious is much more so."[7]

We cite two other figures of indisputable respectability: 1) Arnold Toynbee, who died in 1975 at age 86, characterized in *TIME* Magazine as "an international sage," of the stature of an Einstein, Schweitzer, or Bertrand Russell, and 2) Daisaku Ikeda, President of Soka Gakkai, of the Buddhist League organization, with a membership of thirteen million members in Japan. Both discuss many vital issues, which are part of the current debate about modern man. A publication of their dialogues—*Choose Life*—analyzes in depth the relationship between Reason (Conscious) and Intuition (Non-conscious):

> *Reason and intuition are mutually complementary, in the sense that the former proposes the function of the second, in the sense that one is rectified and clarified by the other. The repeated functioning of the faculty of reason can systematize and elucidate knowledge acquired by means of intention. Although reason, in general,*

6.   Lancelot L. Whyte, *The Unconscious Before Freud*. London: Tavistock Publications, 1960, p. 35

7.   Personal communication with Stephen G. Gillian, reported in his *Therapeutic Trances*, 1978, p.27

adopts an analytic focus and breaks complicated questions into simple, constituent elements, intuition learns about the issue as a whole and penetrates directly into its essential nature. However, although it may seem that the two are opposed one to another, I find that both are aspects related with human wisdom that produce an enriching effect on the nature of man.

The data of sensory perception constitute the prime material of scientific hypotheses. An hypothesis is a provisional explanation of these data.... What is the origin of hypotheses? They are not presented to us by the data of sensory perception. Hypotheses are not data, but rather explanations of data. Neither are they presented by reason. Our rational faculty examines and critiques hypotheses, but does not create them. Reason cannot function until it has an hypothesis with which to work. Reason and perceptions from the senses operate equally at the conscious level of the psyche. Our hypotheses are presented by intuition, from deep within the subconscious. Reason and sensory perceptions are non-creative. The creative activity of the human psyche is intuitive and has its source in the subconscious.[8]

When we analyze the work of thinkers such as Erickson, Rogers, Whyte, Ikeda and Toynbee we learn that our survival depends upon amplifying the range of possible responses to new situations as well as the quality of such responses. In other words, our survival is more and more linked to our potential capacity to become more creative. And creativity, in its turn, does not depend upon our rational, conscious mind, but rather on our unconscious mind.

On the other hand we need the conscious mind; we need *creativity in action*, operational, seeking concrete results. And such creativity can only be derived from an integration of the conscious/unconscious.

In Search of a Theory of Creativity.

When Rogers writes about creativity, he argues that there are at least two preconditions that need to be met if individuals are to activate constructively their creative inspirations:

Condition 1: "When the individual is open to all of his experience, his behavior will be creative and he can have confidence in his creativity as being essentially constructive. To the extent that the individual is open to all aspects of his experience and duly conscious of the varied sensations and perceptions that are registering in the interior of his organism, the new product of his interaction with the environment will tend to be constructive, as much for himself as for others."[9]

---

8.   Arnold Toynbee and Daisaku Ikeda, *Escolha a Vida—Um Diálogo sobre o Futuro*. Rio de Janeiro: Editorial Record, 1976. Pp. 32-33

Condition 2: "If the individual is capable of becoming conscious of his hostile impulses as well as of his desires for friendship and acceptance; if he is capable of being aware of what society expects of him, but also of his personal objectives; if he is capable of becoming conscious of his selfish desires, but also of his sensitivity and concern for others—his behavior will be *harmonious, integrated, constructive.*"

This double affirmation is derived from the experience of Rogers, who dedicated his entire life to psychotherapeutic work. To be creative involves a bringing together of the conscious and unconscious mind, to the opening of a channel between them which permits, via reflection and interpretation, a kind of integration. To use the metaphor previously suggested by Rogers, the creative man is one who is working at the apex of the pyramid, is not isolated from the supporting base, which represents a deeper level. There needs to be an integrative flow between the two, and in the integration of this flow is found to be the essence of the creative act itself.

Ikeda, in his dialogues with Toynbee, affirms that:

> *Consciousness, at a deep level, transcends reason, and can operate with great acuity, rapidity, and precision. Despite the fact that this capacity is inherent in life itself, the development of human civilization has weakened it. In consequence, man came to believe that he can function satisfactorily, even when his conscious capacities at the deep level are inactive. In other words, a superficial human consciousness, including especially rationality, has supplanted the capabilities of a deeper consciousness.*[10]

Toynbee, in his turn, complements the words of Ikeda:

> *There exists a tendency of an older faculty to atrophy when a newer one supplants it. This is too bad, because the new faculty rarely develops all the functions of the old, although it can execute some of them with more efficiency and also uncover new ones that the old never knew nor thought could be done. Among people who have become literate, for example, the faculty of memory weakens, so perhaps literacy, in its turn, will suffer from the use of radio and television as means of communication. In a similar manner, I find the use of the subconscious becoming atrophied in humans by the emphasis on conscious rationality and along with it, reason and culture.*[11]

---

9. Carl Rogers, *op. cit.*
10. Toynbee and Ikeda, *op. cit., p.31*
11. Ibid.

We believe that the challenge we face, in seeking the best way to generate creative individuals, is mainly in the management of the integration between the conscious and the unconscious.

Rogers affirms that, owing to the nature of interior conditions of creativity, it is clear that it cannot be forced, but it becomes enhanced when the person is faced with emergencies. In the same way, a farmer cannot cause a plant to emerge from the seed, but can only create the conditions in which it germinates and develops in all its potentialities.

How can we, then, establish the external conditions, which permit the internal creativity of individuals to be freed up and made to bear its fruits? Rogers proposes two sets of conditions that he called *psychological security and psychological freedom.*

Psychological Security

Psychological security can be obtained by means of three associated strategies:

1. *Acceptance of the individual as an unconditional value:* Whenever a father, professor, mentor, or anyone whose function is to facilitate the growth of others, attributes value to a given individual, independent of his present condition or behavior, he is stimulating the creativity of this individual. This reminds us of the "self-fulfilling prophecy" of McGregor: if you firmly believe that your son or subordinate is capable, that he has the conditions to achieve something, be certain that he will do his best to meet your expectations, whether they be of father, professor, or manager.

2. *Establish a climate in which external evaluation is absent:* When we stop formulating judgments about a person, beginning with the referents of our personal evaluation, we are again favoring creativity. Whether we want to or not, evaluation represents something, which seems threatening, creating an immediate need for a defense! It almost guarantees that a certain part of the experience should be systematically denied to consciousness. In other words, by always emphasizing that the center of evaluation must be exclusively internal to the individual himself, we are creating the basic conditions for his creativity to flourish.

3. *Empathic understanding:* Empathy implies that we see the world with the eyes of others. It is empathic understanding of another which, associated with the above conditions, guarantees the psychological security of the other

person. If the acceptance were merely formal, destitute of any substantive content, without "placing ourselves in the skin of the other," our pseudo-acceptance will be quickly perceived and have exactly a contrary effect, generating insecurities.

Only when the individual feels secure can his real "I" emerge, presenting itself in rich and varied forms. One more time, this favors creativity.

Psychological Freedom

When a professor, parent, therapist, or other person whose function is to facilitate growth permits the individual a complete freedom of symbolic expression, he or she is favoring the emergence of creativity.

It is precisely this freedom, based in belief and confidence that permits one to take certain risks and embark on trails never yet traversed. The result, one more time, is the optimization of the flow of communication between the vast base of the pyramid, representing the unconscious, in the direction of the apex, representing the conscious. The final product is a person whose *creative potential* has been enabled and enhanced.

PART III

Managing the Transpersonal

Chapter 10:
Dealing with the Transcendent

IN SEARCH OF THE SPIRITUAL

For those who have matured and achieved a stage of responsible ego stability, the next stage of growth begins with the transpersonal level, the level of psychic intuition, of transcendent clarity and openness, the awakening of a consciousness that we are more than mere mind and body. In the measure that this begins to happen, there will be profound changes in the society, culture, government, medicine, economy...

—Ken Wilber, *Human Survival and Consciousness Evolution.*

Only you can be your own liberator.

—*Wilhelm Reich*

Ultimately, one cannot justify life and find meaning in it by intellectual analysis and the use of logic. One must reach a state in which he or she experiences emotionally and biologically that it is worthwhile to be alive and feels active excitement about the fact of existence.

—*Stanislav Grof*

What you will find in this chapter

—Introduction to the idea of "extra-conscious"

—The possibility of transcendent experiences

—The nature and conditions of "encounters."

—"Encounters" in themselves.

—The need for spiritual wholeness

Introduction

We have written about managing both the conscious and the unconscious parts of our human potential. Here we turn to what might be called the *"extra-conscious"*—the possibility that we can come to understand and develop the spiritual side of our being. We draw much of the literature used in this section from the work of Stanislav Grof, author of *Beyond the Brain.*[1].

Grof recounts that during the rapid development of humanistic psychology in the 1960s, a new force began to emerge within its inner circle, which emphasized that concepts of "personal growth," and "self-actualization" were too narrow and limited as human developmental objectives. Grof writes:

> *The new emphasis was on recognition of spirituality and transcendental needs as intrinsic aspects of human nature and on the right of every individual to choose or change his or her "path." Many leading humanistic psychologists exhibited a growing interest in a variety of previously neglected areas and topics of psychology, such as mystical experiences, transcendence, ecstasy, cosmic consciousness, theory and practice of meditation, or interindividual and interspecies synergy.*[2]

Jung, a Pioneer

Carl Gustav Jung has been called the first modern psychologist; because only he challenged the prevailing Cartesian-Newtonian worldview—the "positive science" paradigm that has constituted the core of Western philosophical foundations since Newton and Descartes. As June Singer observes, Jung stressed *the importance of the unconscious rather than consciousness, the mysterious rather than the known, the mystical rather than the scientific, the creative rather than the productive, and the religious rather than the profane.*[3]

Jung's image of the human being was not that of a biological machine. Rather, he believed that one can transcend the narrow boundaries of the ego and the per-

---

1. Stanislav Grof, *Beyond the Brain: Birth, Death, and Transcendence in Psychotherapy.* Albany, State University of New York Press, 1985.
2. Stanislav Grof, *Beyond the Brain.* p. 187
3. June Singer, *Boundaries of the Soul: The Practice of Jung's Psychology.* Garden City, NY: Doubleday/Anchor Press, 1972

sonal unconscious to connect with a greater Self that is somehow related with all humanity and the entire cosmos[4]. In contrast to Freud,

> *Jung was willing to accept the irrational, paradoxical, and even mysterious. He had many religious experiences during his lifetime that convinced him of the reality of the spiritual dimension in the universal scheme of things.... Genuine spirituality is an aspect of the collective unconscious and is independent of childhood programming and the individual's cultural or educational background. Thus, if self-exploration and analysis reach sufficient depth, spiritual elements emerge spontaneously into consciousness.*[5]

Building on the earlier work of Jung, Roberto Assagioli, Abraham Maslow and others established a view of psychology that incorporates these potentialities as a distinct sub-discipline called "Transpersonal Psychology" since the 1960s.

Transpersonal Psychology attributes less importance to personality, because for it, man is more than personality, personality being only one of the aspects of being.

> *There is a kind of displacement of inter-psychic and inter-organic aspects "for the recognition of interpersonal relations, family interactions and the social grid. There is also the introduction of economic, ecological and political considerations."*[6]

Transpersonal psychology attempts to include in its body of knowledge all the notions of spirituality of human beings. If we work from Maslow's *Hierarchy of Needs*, we should add at its highest level another level, that of self-transcendence.[7] This would mark a final stage in the development of man.

Learning is a continual process of accumulation, processing and reformulation of information and ideas. The end result is that persons are not only able to see the world with different eyes and to adjust behaviors with respect to the new world they are seeing. Beginning there, the person continues with a process of constructing new knowledge and a search for new ways of acting. We cannot escape the fact that this change in ways of acting presupposes for the individual a

---

4. Grof, p. 188
5. Grof, p. 189
6. Stanislav Grof, *Psychologie Transpersonelle*. Mónaco: du Rocher, 1984, p. 110
7. Geraldo R. Caravantes, *Contexto e Ética: O Perfil do Novo Administrador*. Porto Alegre: FACTEC, 1991. See pages 59-61 for a more complete development of Maslow's theory.

previous change in his/her assumptions, beliefs, and in the consciousness of the individual. In the last analysis:

> *To learn to see the world with different eyes is called a paradigm change, signifying important changes in personal beliefs about how things really function and what are adequate responses in the light of this new understanding.*[8]

Our conclusion is that in the field of administration we need to make a 180° turn in our way of conceiving man in the organization. We have employed a subsystemic notion, partial and non-holistic, to interpret man as less than he effectively is, not creating the minimal conditions necessary for him to expand and utilize his potential, with all the prejudices attendant for the organizations in which they develop their functions.

In the same way, Transpersonal Psychology moves its central focus of attention to the consciousness, making this to be as much the object as the instrument of change. Administrative theory needs to dare to expand its horizons. Traditional personnel administration is no longer sufficient. It needs another framework, another approach which can contemplate consciousness, especially self-reflexive consciousness, since this is the essence of the human being.

In an earlier publication we proposed a new concept we called *Transpersonal Administration*, one that attempts to incorporate this new level of concern that seems to us to be of extreme relevance:

> *A new field of research in administration is contemplated having a multidisciplinary character, where scientific knowledge in areas of Behavior, Applied Behavioral Sciences, Psychology, Cultural Anthropology, Communication, Cybernetics and Strategy, as well as Neurolinguistic Programming and Therapeutic Hypnosis.*[9]

It is not our intention here to paint a complete picture of the development of this view of humans and human potentials. Rather, we simply want to establish some conceptual legitimacy upon which to base what the reader will perceive to be an uncommon approach to the personal development of managers.

---

8.   Geraldo Caravantes and Wesley Bjur, *ReAdministração em Ação*, Op., cit. p. 38

9.   Geraldo R. Caravantes, *Recursos Humanos Estratégicos para o 3° Milênio*. Porto Alegre: CENEX/FACTEC/AGE, 1993, p.46

Touching the Divine

We intend to take up here the possibility for humans to transcend their humanity, to touch the Divine. The possibility of having an actual "encounter" with a spiritual or divine "something" is generally discounted by Western science, but that has not prevented millions of people around the globe from affirming that they have, indeed, experienced such personal encounters.

Particularly in times of crisis, of deepest personal danger or need, the instinct to look "beyond us" in search of superhuman inspiration or strength is a very natural human response. There are innumerable testimonies of persons whose lives have been dramatically changed by the sense of such "encounters." The experience has transformed important elements in their lives. There are many testimonies of how it has given them a special kind of inner (or spiritual) strength in the face of overwhelming personal adversity.

We include a discussion of such experiences in this chapter on personal growth because both authors have had transcendent experiences, of encounters with something "out there," something beyond the ordinary experiences, which have had decisive influence on the focus of our personal and professional lives.

There is admittedly a personal reluctance to reveal such things, partly because they are so intensely personal, and partly because of a fear that they may be held up to ridicule by a professional fraternity which is ostensibly dedicated to rational, scientific management of human and physical resources. Nevertheless, because these personal, transcendent experiences have proven, with the passage of time, to have been pivotal events in the lives of the authors, to fail to recommend them to others who might be similarly benefited could be seen as selfish.

Out of our experience, tempered by a lifetime of reading and study of the evolution of movements to enhance human potential and development, we propose to discuss more fully:

1. **the possibility of transcendent, or spiritual, experiences,**

2. **the nature and conditions of what we call "encounters,"**

3. **the context in which such encounters generally occur, and**

4. **the metaphoric nature of extra-rational "encounters."**

1. The Possibility of the Transcendent

We affirm that human experience regularly transcends the rational. To name only a few examples of extra-rational human phenomena:

—The very fine *basic human qualities* that include conscience, guilt, idealism, spirituality, patriotism, artistic expression, and others are extra-rational in spirit and in expression.

—*Falling in love* is certainly not a rational activity, but who would deny its importance?

—The *creative arts* defy rational explanation, both in their inspiration and in their aesthetic expression. Painting, sculpture, poetry, and music—all have extra-rational elements. The unexplained "link-up" between individual jazz musicians when they are creating an unrehearsed and unscored performance serves as an example of ways in which humans regularly transcend rational states of being. Art, being at the same time a representation of reality and a denial of it, presents the mind with a non-rational ambiguity which can be only personally resolved.

—*Reveries, dreams, myths*—after researching certain universal mythological motifs around the world, Jung concluded that there are myth-forming structural elements in the unconscious psyche that give rise to the fantasy lives and dreams of individuals and to the mythology of peoples. Dreams can thus be seen as individual myths, and myths as collective dreams.[10]

2. The Nature and Conditions of "Encounter" Experiences

There seem to be some pre-requisites associated with accounts of personal encounters with that Something-Beyond-Us that can be classified as encounters with the Divine. First of all, it seems inevitably a solitary experience, associated with facing a problem or dilemma alone. It definitely is NOT a group experience.

Secondly, it often grows out of a reflective or meditative stance, a seeking or searching for an understanding of events or circumstances whose explanation eludes our rational capabilities. Why *this*? Why *me*? Why *now*?

---

10.   Grof, p. 189

Thirdly, there is usually an awareness of personal insufficiency to deal with the problem being faced, a recognition which leads to the search for an enlightenment that comes from beyond our natural, rational understanding.

Fourthly, the insight from "beyond us," when it comes, is often somewhat "fuzzy" or shadowy in its presentation in the mind, requiring further interpretation from within the personal experience of the "encountered one" in order to fully understand, with the help of intuition and the rational mind, its complete significance. The "message" may be figurative, as in the form of an image, or it may be as intelligible words registering in the mind. However, it may often be cryptically brief, needing metaphoric interpretation in the light of personal interpretation and understanding of its content and meaning.

Despite its ambiguity, it yet carries an enduring and powerful message to the hearer, oft times one with life-long significance.

3. The Context of "Encounters"

Most adults, trained and habituated to operate from within rational parameters, are not accustomed to consult their transcendent potentials. It is only when faced with some important transition from the known to the unknown, from the familiar to the unfamiliar (and therefore feared) that one recognizes the need to call upon untapped resources.

Uncertainty, ambiguity, and frustration associated with workplace assignments can stress to the limits of personal resources, until there seems to be no where to turn. Life-threatening accidents or serious illness, loss of partner or spouse, loss of family and friends, loss of one's employment—all can be serious blows to one's sense of stability, wholeness, and ability to survive the onslaught of life's travails. Under such circumstances who would not cry out to some unseen power, some spiritual life force, for sustenance?

4. The Metaphoric Nature of the Encounter

More than three decades ago philosopher of science Jacques Ellul wrote, *"Science gives a metaphor."* He was one of the early ones to point out the fallacy of believing that so-called scientific knowledge can, in any way, approach the idea of being a faithful copy in the human mind of a physical reality exterior to us.

Thus, to transcend the limits of our physical senses is to enter territory where the vocabulary of the physical world no longer serves to describe experiences. We are left to speak in metaphors—to "feel" and "understand" the experience more fully in the "heart of hearts" than we are able to describe it to others, or even understand it ourselves.

The Symbolic Nature of Knowing

In Part I we discussed Cassirer's "symbolic theory of knowledge" which, since the Kantian revolution, has replaced the naive idea that True Knowledge exists as a True Copy in the human mind of the physical reality out there, exterior to us. That the mind could ever possess a faithful copy of external reality has been demonstrated impossible in uncounted physiological tests. Rather, our minds hold their images of external reality in the form of symbolic representations, which we create for ourselves out of the memory residues of sensory impressions reaching the mind from sense organs. Just as the magnetic smudges recorded on a Mylar tape represent images reproduced by a modern video camera-recorder, so the memories of sights and sounds are recorded in one's unique, symbolic way for recovery by memory. What must be emphasized is the recorded images are *not a faithful copy of the sensory streams, but our own personalized, symbolic representation of how we perceived them.*

In other words, all human knowledge consists of our personally constructed symbol systems for remembering what has happened in the past. The sensory streams themselves have no meaning to us until we have turned them into symbolic representations of something, which has meaning for us. Thus, it is true to affirm that ALL human knowledge is a personally derived symbolic representation of what each of us *believes* to have occurred. A symbolic representation is another name for a metaphor: something, which stands for something else.

So if all human knowledge, including that of the physical sciences, is in reality metaphoric, it will not then seem strange that we can speak of transcendent experiences only in metaphoric terms.

The Encounter Itself

So permit us to speak in metaphoric terms of four "encounters" with what we call the Divine, personally experienced by the two authors. All four grew out of personal crises—events which threw into question the understanding of answers to life-long questions: *"Who am I?"* and *"What ought I to do with my life?"*

Encounter 1 [Bjur]

"In my late 'teens I felt I had a vocational calling to live and work as a teacher overseas. A decade later, now married, I applied for affiliation with an organization sponsoring such work, and was ordered to submit to a rigorous physical examination as one of the conditions of employment. To my surprise, the examining physician reported that I had a heart murmur, and he therefore could not recommend extended overseas living.

"This news quite destroyed my vision of who I was [*not* sickly] as well as what was my calling and destiny in adulthood. In effect, it completely aborted my carefully constructed vision of how I had intended to spend the rest of my life. I consulted friends and counselors on whom I had previously depended, but got no illumination. Left to my own resources, I spent the next six months in a solitary, agonizing, spiritual search for answers to the most basic questions of who I was, and what I should do with my life. This agonizing search was the preparation to my first encounter with what I am calling the Divine.

"Subsequent to the "encounter" my heart murmur disappeared, and soon after we were accepted for an overseas assignment. What was for me a transcendent experience gave new direction to my life and resulted in moving our family to Chile, South America where we lived and worked for the next decade. There we became immersed in a different culture, and learned Spanish as a second language. Our children were schooled in *L'Alliance Française*, which meant that as parents we also needed to learn French (as a third language) in order to help them with schoolwork. We traveled to other Latin American republics; Argentina, Paraguay, Perú, Bolivia, Cuba and Central America, with opportunities to see and experience other cultures first hand. We dealt with political and cultural elites, but also with the economically disadvantaged. We taught young children, also university students and adults. We coped with political uprisings, rampant inflation, a sense of alienation and a numbing nostalgia, especially at Christmas time, which happens in the middle of summer in the Southern Hemisphere.

"As I matured in age and experience in Chile, I grew into greater leadership and administrative responsibilities. In sum, that decade was a most important part of my formation as a person and a professional. That international experience became the base upon which my later university and consulting career was built. Goals, values, habits, relationships growing out of that experience became so much a part of my character that I cannot imagine my later professional life without that experience of maturing in another culture."

Encounters 2 and 3

"There were important differences between the first encounter, described above, and the second and third, both of which grew out of accidents involving serious physical trauma to our oldest son. As his father, I had to make decisions affecting the outcome of his medical treatments. One accident occurred when he was a child; the second when he was thirty and was nearly killed in a terrible freeway accident. Each of the encounters was so intensely personal that I hesitate to speak of them to this day. I can only say that through each encounter I received personal assurance, or what might be called "advance information" as to what I should do, or how things would evolve, an assurance that brought a special kind of peace and confidence in the face of overwhelming anguish and anxiety.

"I report these personal experiences as examples of the type of extra-personal growth that can occur in maturing persons who are willing to engage themselves in a concerted search for a reality deeper than the superficial world in which we live. My search was made easier by early parental and religious training, which motivated me to persist until I met the Divine (or He met me?). That training included a vocabulary for understanding the nature of transcendent experiences, along with illustrations from Biblical literature about encounters experienced by others since ancient times."

Carl Jung studied accounts of similar experiences recounted by people from other cultures and religions around the world. The vocabulary used to describe their perceptions of the experiences varies among different regions, religions and cultures, but the profound effects on the individual tend to be similar. Almost without exception it is a maturing experience, one imparting a new and deep sense of being at peace with oneself and with the Life Force of the universe. Often there grows a new sense of self-confidence, a belief that things will turn out all right, that the person will be able to cope successfully with the traumatizing events and emerge on the other side with one's ego strengthened by the struggle.

Encounter 4: "Lui, Il Parle Français!"[11] [Caravantes]

"Some years ago, in 1976 to be exact, I was in London participating in a postgraduate program in the Royal Institute of Public Administration (RIPA), a program designed to improve the effectiveness of a select group of government executives from several countries. During the months that I was there several

---

11.   "He speaks French!"

interesting and relevant things were going on, including contact with the team that works with John Humble, who was then developing in Europe a research and consultation associated with *Management By Objectives*. That contact inspired me to produce my first book, published in 1977.[12] The contact with a group from the Tavistock Institute in London introduced me to the relevance of the socio-technical approach as a healthier, intelligent, and effective way to interpret organizational phenomena.

"The curricular program of the Royal Institute, well concatenated and planned, presented a vision not merely of European administration, but also that of other countries—many of them ex-British colonies—who were then resolving their own problems associated with administrative development.

"However, while these good things were going on, a specific, personal and professional problem related to a decision that I needed to make kept hammering at my consciousness: "What should I do upon my return?" Continue in the public service? Continue in the University (I was recently contracted to the faculty of the Federal University)? Or should I accept a good proposal coming from the private sector, or work in another Brazilian city? Or, who knows, perhaps develop my own business that might bring better financial opportunities to earn money, according to the degree of importance that this meant? It was important to keep in consideration that we are speaking of someone thirty years old, with four children, recently having moved from Rio de Janeiro, attempting to relocate in a new environment.

"What should I do?" was the question that hammered at my mind continually. The ideas contained in the text, *Personal Planning*, already referred to, was an autodidactic resource that helped, giving me a certain rational organization to my ways of thinking and to the search, in this phase, even though that text was not published until a year later. Meanwhile, a response to my search emerged in a way a bit prosaic.

"Upon the termination of the course in London, and before returning to Brazil, I decided to go to Paris. The same night that I arrived there—it was almost midnight—I decided to take a stroll along the shores of the Seine, to see some of the *bouquinistes* (obviously closed, given the advanced hour of the night) and to localize the Sorbonne University.

---

12. I refer to Geraldo R. Caravantes, *Administração Por Objetivos: Uma Abordagem Sócio-técnica,* published by McGraw-Hill, with a preface by Luiz Simóes Lopes, President of the Getulio Vargas Foundation, something of which I am justifiably proud.

"With a fragmentary map, but with a fair understanding of French and of the city (knowledge acquired through books, not first hand, since it was my first visit to Paris) and with a certain mixture of apprehension and marveling, I decided what I wanted to do. It was a spontaneous choice, because it was about one o'clock in the morning, in a relatively cool night. I was the only person walking along these narrow streets, marked by secular construction that that reminded me of a Paris I knew only from literature, but which seemed to me kind of like an old friend.

"Shortly after passing in front of the Sorbonne, and admiring it for some time, as I was preparing to return, I heard the strains of soft music coming from an organ. It seemed to me a bit unusual, almost magic, and I walked towards the flow of the music. I ended up finding a small church, Gothic in style, from where the music was emanating. Since the doors were open, I entered and seated myself in the very last bench. The only illumination was from a small lamp near the altar, yielding an orange glow, and another lamp next to the organ. In the moments that I was there I was hearing Bach and Beethoven, and some Gregorian Chants. I confess that I was enraptured with what I was experiencing. I was certain that something like this happens only once in a lifetime.

"When the music ended (it must have been 1:30 or 2:00 in the morning) my conscious mind returned to the initial question— *"What should I do upon my return?"* It was just then as if Someone,—the name is not important,—whispered in my ear the response to my inquiries. And it was done in a simple and direct way, but also with high style. In the French language, *sans aucun doûte:*

"Faire suffisament d'argent d'un travail intellectuel."[13]

"I rapidly got hold of my pen and made a note on a small pad I always carried with me. This experience has had a profound influence on the course of my life since then. The University career itself—with the decision to earn a Masters degree, a Doctorate, and subsequently a Post-doctorate—all stem from that experience.

The Spiritually Enriched Manager

To summarize what we have been saying throughout this chapter, the authors, based upon personal experience and supported by the testimony of many others, have observed that persons who have been tested to their limits by adversity, to a point of crying out in anguish of soul for help from beyond their own resources,

---

13. "Earn enough money [to do] intellectual work."

can somehow touch a more-than-human source, a wellspring of moral strength that will enable them to carry on in the face of unbelievable difficulties.

A really mature manager, one who can face unexpected reverses and still show calmness and a deep strength of character, emerges from this kind of testing. Spiritual resources carry them through, resources discovered while on their knees, bowed down in anguish of body and soul, only to be restored to their feet by a touch from the Divine. The experience both humbles and strengthens. Most importantly, its strength endures, a strength that can appear manifested in many facets of one's life.

Personal plus Professional Growth

We affirm that it is important for managers to grow as persons in parallel with their growth as professionals. In fact, the longer one's managerial experience, the higher one moves in the organization, the more likely it is that some experiences similar to what we describe here shall have contributed to overall maturity and personal development. At different times in their personal and professional lives leaders feel the need to *transcend* the rationalistic and physical barriers of their human existence in order to reach out and touch the Divine. In our experience, such encounters make them stronger and better persons, enabling them to attain higher levels of managerial leadership.

We have defended the idea that high-performance organizations are the result of the fact that they possess, in their work force, people who are both happy and actualized.[14] The argument can also be stated inversely: people unhappy and unactualized, with *lowered* effectiveness, can only bring to the organization what they are and what they have to offer: their own unhappiness and a narrowed, reduced functioning.

New Research on Spiritual Wholeness

Evidence supporting the need for fostering a sense of spiritual wholeness in employees has recently been published by Mitroff and Denton, highly regarded researchers of organizational theory and practice, in "*A Spiritual Audit of Corporate America*." They sent 2000 questionnaires to Human Resources executives of U.S. corporations, and personally interviewed several dozen chief executives of

---

14. For a discussion of the two concepts: "happiness," and "actualized," see Geraldo Caravantes and Wesley Bjur, *ReAdministração em Ação,* Chapter 1.

East-and West Coast American corporations. The researchers defined spirituality by asking what the term meant to individuals who were interviewed. Among many responses, here is one that seemed widely shared:

> *Spirituality is the ultimate source and provider of meaning and purpose in our lives. It satisfies a deep hunger and yearning in all of us for meaning and purpose. This sense of personal meaning is reinforced by the notion that the universe itself is not meaningless, that it is not devoid of purpose, that there is a supreme being who is the source of all life, existence, meaning and purpose.*[15]

Mitroff and Denton write that most of those to whom they spoke had experienced some form of "wounding of the soul" as a result of working in organizations. This was the case whether the organization was for-profit or not-for-profit.[16] By "wounding of the soul," the interviewees were referring to being forced to suppress or to violate some of their deeply held values in service of company policies. Another kind of "wounding" was related to the feeling of being treated as robots, as non-entities, of not being able to express themselves as whole persons, of spending their working hours in meaningless activities.

> *The hands-down, first choice of everyone we interviewed regarding what gave them the most meaning and purpose in their job was "the ability to realize my full potential as a person." In extremely close second place was "being associated with a good organization" or "being associated with an ethical organization…" The third choice was having "interesting work" while a distant fourth was "making money."*[17]

In a world rapidly becoming globalized, high quality and efficient production are not merely desirable—they are now a condition of survival. Entrepreneurs, administrators, executives and the organizations they have created need to understand and use the power of the spiritual, the transcendent, for themselves as well as for their employees. Executives become the ones who must expand in response to needs and opportunities. This seems to us to be the way, possibly the *only* way, to survive and thrive in the new century. To quote the recent work of Mitroff and Denton once more:

---

15. Ian I. Mitroff and Elizabeth Denton, *A Spiritual Audit of Corporate America: Spirituality, Religion and Values in the Workplace.* San Francisco: Jossey-Bass Publishers. 1999 p.24
16. Mitroff and Denton, *op. cit.,* p.46
17. Mitroff and Denton, *op. cit.,* p.36

All organizations, for-profits as well as not-for-profits, need to learn how to harness the immense spiritual energies of their members if they are to become both ethical and profitable over the long haul. Any organization can make money in the short run by exploiting and maltreating its employees, but if it wishes to be profitable over the long haul, it needs to learn how to be spiritual.[18]

18.　Mitroff and Denton, *op. cit.,* p.48

Chapter 11:
Some Concluding Thoughts about Managing with Magic

By declaring that man is responsible and must actualize the potential meaning of his life, I wish to stress that the true meaning of life is to be discovered in the world rather than within man or his own psyche, as though it were a closed system. I have termed this constitutive characteristic "the self-transcendence of human existence."... What is called self-actualization is not an attainable aim at all, for the simple reason that the more one would strive for it, the more he would miss it. In other words, self-actualization is possible only as a side effect of self-transcendence.

—Victor Frankl, Man's Search for Meaning.

What you will find in this chapter

1. **How to view the manager as magician**

2. **A culture without magic**

3. **Magic as a "natural" part of nature**

4. **Man as an "extendable" being**

5. **The duty to be happy**

The Manager As "Magician"

We began this book listing various possible ways to interpret the term, "magic" and "magician," without discussing or explaining in any deeper sense what we are implying by the choice of the word. The idea was to construct a learning process, one designed to assist personal growth and self-confidence, hoping that at the end the reader himself shall have arrived at his own conclusions. In a certain way, this was part of the "play" of the magician in the book.

Here are some of our own interpretations about the contemporary use of the idea of "magic" so that the reader might have some idea of how our reasoning evolved:

- —Magic as the management of the scenario.

- —Magic as the management of impressions.

- —Magic as the intelligent use of science.

- —Magic as the act of planning, preparing and conducting a performance.

- —Magic as the performance in itself:
    —performance as an "efficient" organizational production
    —performance as the development of leadership;
    —performance as the presentation of a "show," where the values
      of the company and its products are presented.

At base, what we really desired was to show that for administrators in particular—pragmatic by professional training and oriented towards action—as well as for readers in general, there exist other ways to perceive the world and to cope with it, ways different from those in which we have been habituated. In the words of Thomas Moore:

> *For us, the act of understanding something about the world moves us, permanently, to application; we translate science into technology. Thus, generally we involve ourselves in exploration, using without measure the existing materials of the world for our own narcissistic purposes. Finally, all of this carries us to abuse of nature and of people, in the measure of which we use both, for the compulsive advance of a culture without magic.*[1]

And what is the alternative to this almost suicidal approach that today prevails, adopted at the planetary level? Thomas Moore himself suggests a new way:

---

1.   Thomas Moore, *The Re-Enchantment of Everyday Life*. New York: Harper Comrigs, 1990 p. XIII.

The approach of magic is different from that which to which we are accustomed to use to cope with the world…The alternative which it proposes is to translate science into a marveling, a philosophy, history, and to an intimacy with nature. In place of excesses of exploitation we can come to value simplicity of life; reserve in our use of people and things, and respect for the limitations which nature imposes on us. Instead of being obsessive in disseminating modern culture around the globe, and projecting it into the future, we can take into account that other cultures have much to teach us, and that the Third World is, in many areas, more advanced and sophisticated than is ours [USA]. We can have the modesty to question our own advances, and the humility to learn from others. Magic offers a rationale little used, but profound, to help us to adopt an ecological posture in our day-to-day living.[2]

Magic As a Part of Nature

What we propose is that magic does not consist in the external, neither in the extraordinary, but rather in a return to the basic and the essential that is found inside of ourselves. It is discovered in self-knowledge, in simplicity, and in our connections with nature. It is discovered while taking into awareness that such expressions as *"the dominance of nature by man"* or *"man versus nature"* are foolish, a product of our failure to reflect upon the characteristics of our humanness. Ultimately, man is an integral and essential part of nature itself. Alan Watts writes:

What we really are, in the first place, is all of our body. However, the body is covered with a skin—I am capable of differentiating the external from my internal—my body cannot exist except as a determined species in a natural environment. Obviously, it requires air, and this air should be within a determined temperature range; it requires nutrition, it requires that it be on a certain type of planet, proximate to a certain type of star that rotates regularly in a rhythmic and harmonic manner, in a form that life can be maintained. Such an arrangement is necessary to the existence of my body, as well as all of my internal organs—my heart, my brain, my lungs, and so on. In this way, there is no way to separate me, with respect to my physical body, from the natural environment in which I live.[3]

We believe that magic consists in recognizing ourselves as integrated and participant beings in nature, and not distinct nor separate from it, and never *against* nature. We are uncompleted beings in a process that can—or perhaps can-

---

2.   Ibid.
3.   Allan Watts, *The Essential of Alan Watts*. Berkeley, California: Celestial Arts, 1977, p. 34

not—come to fulfill their potential, becoming all that they have the possibility and conditions to be.

Man as an "extendable" being

Only when we no longer perceive ourselves as contained and limited by the walls of the "container," i.e., our physical body, but rather compared with the waters of the ocean, with all of its vastness, mystery, and infinite possibilities, can we make a positive difference for ourselves and for humanity. Again from Thomas Moore:

> *If such reflections and suggestions seem ingenuous and non-operational, in a neurotic culture oriented towards its own productivity and self-growth, a reason might be that we believe ourselves to be incapable of exercising control over the machinery of our hyperactivity. For example: we have made evolution into a god, accepting it not merely as a scientific rule, but rather as a necessity that cannot be halted, impeded, or modified. While we recognize our responsibility to humanize our culture, appealing to the inexorability of evolution…Yet, for us, evolution has come to be not only a theory, but an imperative that cannot be questioned.*[4]

However, both authors hold positive views of the world, of humanity, and of the future. Both believe that the organizational society we have created, is viable. Both also share in another idea, that only free individuals, educated, with broadened potentials, reflexive and happy about themselves, can create a viable new society. Such a society is made up of persons who cultivate continued learning as the proper condition of their survival, as well as that of society as a whole.

The Duty To Be Happy

The Argentine poet, Jorge Luiz Borges wrote: *"We have the duty to be happy, but we do not achieve it."* In an organizational world, the leaders/administrators of organizations are those who have the responsibility, the non-delegable responsibility, for making possible this condition of happiness[5] to which all of us aspire.

---

4.   Thomas Moore, *op. cit.*
5.   The authors have a book in progress to develop philosophical and practical insights about the nature of the responsibility managers have to guarantee a special kind of individual and corporate happiness in the organization that employs them. In other words, managers are, in some ways, responsible for their own happiness, as well as that of the employees they manage.

About the Author

Wesley E. Bjur Ph.D., Emeritus Associate Professor, University of Southern California. Professor Bjur moved with his family to Chile in 1953, returning in 1964 to graduate studies. He joined the faculty of the University of Southern California as Director of their International Public Administration Center in 1966. In 1973 he was sent as Chief of Party to initiate an Institute of Urban and Regional Development in México, returning in 1975 to continue research and teaching on international development management and administrative change. United Nations, USAID, and Latin American Development Bank contracted Bjur as a consultant in Africa, Asia, and Latin America. He served as Senior Fulbright Lecturer in Madrid 1990, returning to Madrid 1993-96 to teach graduate courses in modern administrative theory and practice. Married 50+ years, the Bjurs make their home in Sacramento, California living near a married daughter and four of 12 grandchildren.

Geraldo R. Caravantes Ph.D., Emeritus Professor, Universidade Federão do Rio Grande do Sul, ex-President of Research Foundation FAPERGS. Professor Caravantes has published 16 books on management, strategic planning, theories of administration, and related topics. He travels widely as lecturer and consultant to Brazilian universities and large corporations. He has delivered more than 450 seminars on executive development throughout Brazil, and has lectured and taught in Madrid and the United States. Married 30+ years, the Caravantes make their home in Porto Alegre, R.S. Brazil, where they enjoy the companionship of four married children and grandchildren.

0-595-27104-9